Seven Heretical Sermons

Seven Heretical Sermons

David Davis

BOOKLOGIX
Alpharetta, Georgia

Although the author has made every reasonable effort to ensure that the information in this book is correct, the author does not assume and hereby disclaims any liability to any party for any loss, damage, or disruption caused by errors or omissions, whether such errors or omissions result from negligence, accident, or any other cause.

Copyright © 2023 by David Davis

All rights reserved. No part of this book may be reproduced or transmitted in any form or by any means, electronic or mechanical, including photocopying, recording, or any information storage and retrieval system, without permission in writing from the author.

ISBN: 978-1-6653-0651-5 - Paperback
ISBN: 978-1-6653-0652-2 - Hardcover
eISBN: 978-1-6653-0653-9 - ePub

These ISBNs are the property of BookLogix for the express purpose of sales and distribution of this title. The content of this book is the property of the copyright holder only. BookLogix does not hold any ownership of the content of this book and is not liable in any way for the materials contained within. The views and opinions expressed in this book are the property of the Author/Copyright holder, and do not necessarily reflect those of BookLogix.

Library of Congress Control Number: 2023911398

⊚This paper meets the requirements of ANSI/NISO Z39.48-1992 (Permanence of Paper)

Scripture quotations taken from the New English Bible, copyright © Cambridge University Press and Oxford University Press 1961, 1970. All rights reserved.

070523

Contents

Note from the Author — *vii*

Sermon One
  Beginnings — 1
Sermon Two
  Purpose — 13
Sermon Three
  Abortion — 33
Sermon Four
  Homosexuality — 47
Sermon Five
  Evil — 71
Sermon Six
  The Last Supper — 79
Sermon Seven
  God — 93

Acknowledgments — *103*

Note from the Author

I have used the literary form of a sermon (direct address to a group on a topic related to religion or morality) to try to simplify and make clear what are often complex topics. However, some of these sermons are far too long to ever be preached during a regular church service. If they have any use at all, it is to prompt thought, and perhaps discussion, of some of these topics. My aim is to cause those used to more conventional approaches to religious ideas to look at things slightly differently. Hence, these are not explanations of scripture but discussions of topics that scripture has been applied to by some.

The ideas expressed are neither new nor original. The theological ideas can be found in dozens of modern books and articles. The ideas taken from anthropology come mostly from popularizers of anthropology, such as the series of books by Jared Diamond or the works of Nicholas Wade, both of whom are synthesizing and simplifying the ideas and research of other academics. So again, nothing is original to me. The concepts from physics and other sciences are found in any college-level text on the subject.

Biblical quotations are generally from the New English Bible, unless otherwise noted, with the exception that I have leaned heavily on Robert Alter's translation of the first five books of the bible, mainly because of its glorious footnotes explaining the issues he faced in translating certain passages.

Sermon One

Beginnings

Today, I want to talk about how religion started. Now, I'm not talking about the birth of Jesus, or when Abraham and Sarah got together, or when the Egyptian Book of the Dead was compiled, or even when the story of Gilgamesh was being told around Sumerian campfires. Today, we go way back, tens of thousands of years ago.

Now, just to give you a little perspective, Jesus was walking around Galilee about two thousand years ago. David was king of Israel about three thousand years ago. Abraham and Moses are a good deal more difficult to date because we're not sure how much is fact and how much is legend, but we're still only talking four or five thousand years ago, maybe six thousand on the outside. Writing was invented about five thousand years ago, so even the stories and legends orally preserved and then written down later only go back a few thousand years more at most.

So, when I say we're talking about tens of thousands of years ago, we're going way back—back so far there were still two or three kinds of human beings alive, because there were still Neanderthals, and maybe Denisovans, walking around, along with *Homo sapiens*. Now for those of you not up on your anthropological classifications, *Homo sapiens* is us—modern humans. We're past all the *Australopithecus* and *Homo habilis* here. All those fun people died out millions of years ago. We're talking about our five hundred or thousand times great-grandfathers, but we're still talking *us*.

I don't want to get too hung up on the dates here—first of all, because we don't know exactly when it happened; it probably happened gradually, it may have happened more than once in different places, and the exact date really doesn't matter. What really matters for this discussion is that some tens of thousands of years ago, something changed, and that something is a sign, an indicator, that religion had started.

Now, I guess first we have to define what we mean by religion. We are not talking about a particular religion, like Islam or Christianity or Hinduism or Judaism; we are talking about a belief that there is something beyond this life—gods, an afterlife, whatever. That's all we're talking about: the belief that there is something else. What the people way back then thought that something else was, we can't know for sure, but we think they must have thought there was something.

The reason we think that is that when we look at fossils of all those types of humans who came before us—the *Homo ergasters* and *Homo heidelbergenisis*, etc.—on those very rare occasions when we find their fossils, it's just like finding the fossil of an ape or other big mammal; something that survived by pure chance. Maybe there was a mudslide that killed a whole bunch of animals and then preserved their bones as fossils; or a volcanic eruption whose piles of ash preserved the shapes of the bones of whatever died that day. There aren't many ways to get a fossil to form and hang around for millions of years, but when we do find one of somebody on the tree of human ancestors, it's usually no different from the other animal fossils lying around.

What this tells us is that, generally speaking, human bodies pretty much got left where they died, just like other animals did and still do today. Scavenger animals like vultures and hyenas (not to mention all kinds of bugs) come along and eat everything that isn't bone, usually scattering the bones around a bit, and if somehow those bones become fossils, that's what we find—scattered, often broken, bones.

But several tens of thousands of years ago, for humans, that began to change. From that period, we begin to find human bodies that weren't just left but buried. And this wasn't just digging a hole and dumping the body in or piling a mound of dirt over it to keep all those scavenger hyenas and vultures away. We find bones that look like the bodies were placed, the graves oriented to the track of the sun or some other notable celestial object. And sometimes several bodies from the same place and the same time would be placed in the same positions, maybe curled up like a fetus or laid flat on their backs, even side by side. And, most notably, sometimes these bodies would be buried with what are called "grave goods": a good stone hand axe, a necklace made of shells, clothing they were wearing, maybe even some kind of container with food in it, that kind of thing. Things we think that person probably used during their life.

Now, the question is why would the living do that with their dead? Hand axes are hard to make—chipping one stone against another so one flakes into a sharp edge. Those shells in the necklace may have come from hundreds of miles away, being traded from group to group for other valuable items. Clothing was made from animal skins, which meant you had to kill some big animal first, skin it, dry the skin, cut it, and then find some way to hang it and hold it on your body. The point is that these were valuable, hard-to-get things that the people who were still alive could have used. Again, why would they put these things in a grave?

Now, of course, they are not around to tell us, and they hadn't invented writing yet, so they didn't leave any books on the significance of their funeral traditions. But if we look at what people wrote tens of thousands of years later and talk to people who were still getting by using stone tools until just a few decades ago, which some anthropologists did, we can make an educated guess. They believed the dead would need those objects in whatever came after death.

I want to be very careful here. Our ancestors from way back then may have been primitive, but they weren't stupid. Their brains were actually slightly bigger than ours. They knew an awful lot about the world they lived in. They knew about the migrations of the animals. They knew that the seasons and the movement of the sun and stars were related somehow. They knew which animals you could stampede over a cliff and which would more likely turn and charge right at you. They knew how to stay alive. They also probably knew death really well. They didn't have nursing homes or funeral directors. They killed and butchered their own meat. They watched death come and they dealt with the bodies left behind. They didn't believe that if you buried somebody and came back later and dug them up, the body would be gone. They knew better than that. They knew the body and whatever else was in that grave would still be there unless some animal or grave robber dug them up first.

But we think they believed that there was, for lack of a better term, a "spirit world" of some kind. Some "spirit" of the person would go on to the spirit world, taking the spirit of the axe, necklace, clothing, and food for the journey with them. So, these burials and grave goods are evidence of a religion, a belief that there was something else, something beyond. So, we can say with some assurance that, by this time, religion has started.

But that only brings us to our next question: Why would our ancestors reach the conclusion that there is something else besides this life? What made them decide that they needed to bury their dead in preparation for this something else? And here I am going to have to pause again to explain how I am going to use certain terms, namely "dreams," "hallucinations," and "visions." I want to keep certain concepts separate, so I'm using these words a little more narrowly than usual.

Dreams are what happens in our brains while we are asleep. They come and go during the night or during naps. Sometimes, we will remember part of a dream that we are having just before we wake up, but most dreams pass without notice. Maybe dreams are our brains reprogramming themselves, replaying events of the day and tying them into related mental linkages. Maybe dreams are our subconscious wrestling with problems or issues and trying to work things out. Maybe they are just images and memories being brought up and jammed together at random.

And, of course, we're not the only animal that dreams. Apes dream, even dogs dream. They go through the same stages of sleep, the same rapid eye movements during dream cycles, the same twitching and tossing. Now, what dogs dream about is not totally clear; maybe they are dreaming about chasing squirrels or cars or about curling up in front of a nice, warm fireplace, or about their master giving them a big, raw sirloin steak instead of another bowl of dog chow. We haven't figured out a way to get them to tell us yet, though one day we might be able to read their brainwaves or something.

But the point is, dreams are something that happens to most big mammals, including us. And when we wake up and realize we have been having a dream, we don't think it was real. It might be our subconscious trying to tell us something or even possibly a message from some god or ancestor, but the dream itself was just a dream, not reality. And we know that.

Hallucinations, on the other hand, happen when we are awake. They seem real at the time, and it's only later, looking back on it, that we realize that it wasn't as real as we thought. There are lots of ways to have a hallucination. Several kinds of mental illnesses, such as schizophrenia, are characterized by hallucinations. There are drugs and chemicals in plants that can induce hallucinations. People who become extremely—and I do mean *extremely*—exhausted or sleep-deprived or dehydrated or close to death sometimes experience hallucinations. Whatever the cause, people who have had hallucinations report that at the time it all seemed very real. They believe that what they were seeing and hearing was real, actually happening. Only afterward, after the drug wore off or the mental illness got treated or the exhaustion or sleeplessness got dealt with, were they able to look back and say it wasn't real.

And then there are the events that I am using the term "vision" to describe. It's a good religious word: a visual and auditory experience of the divine. We talk about Paul's vision on the road to Damascus, Moses's vision of the burning bush, John's vision of heaven in Revelations. A very religious word. The thing about a vision is that it seems very real when it is happening, and even afterward, the person who experienced it still believes it really happened, even if it broke a few laws of physics and violated what we generally consider to be the way reality works.

Paul certainly believed he really met and talked to Jesus on the road to Damascus, even if Jesus was not only dead and resurrected but even ascended to heaven. All his actions and theology, his claims to authority, were based on his belief that his vision was an experience of reality. Later, he writes about knowing a man, possibly himself, who ascended to a couple of levels of heaven, looked around, then came back down. He says he doesn't know if this man ascended bodily or in the spirit, but he doesn't question that what that man saw in heaven was real. Likewise, Moses never questioned that his burning bush was real, and Peter, James, and John evidently never questioned that they actually saw Moses and Elijah talking to Jesus up on the mountain.

Now, visions, in this sense of both seeming real at the time and believed to be real later, despite not fitting into normal reality, are not unique to Christianity and Judaism. Muhammad spent some time talking to an angel. The Buddha evidently had a vision or two. And visions are not limited to people who end up starting religions. There have been mystics through the ages, in almost all religions and cultures, that have reported visions and messages from God. But that's another sermon.

Let's get back to our question about why our ancestors so long ago evidently decided that there was something after death that could somehow be improved if the dead were buried in a certain way or provided with certain items to take with them into the grave. Now, like I said, these people were primitive but not stupid. I very strongly suspect that they dreamed at night the same way we do now, probably about the same kind of things: sex, food, power—that kind of thing, only in Stone Age terms. But I suspect they also knew a dream was just a dream, at most some kind of symbolic message from beyond, not a reality.

But if we ask the healers and medicine men in the very primitive societies that first encountered civilization in the past couple of hundred years (which anthropologists did) what they were doing to heal people or ensure a successful hunt, what they say, drastically oversimplified, is that they are inducing a vision that allows them to travel to the spirit world to get rid of bad spirits or get information from the spirits of their ancestors. These visions can be induced by dancing for hours on end, or staying awake for days, or eating or drinking or smoking concoctions from certain plants, or some combination thereof.

What I am suggesting here—and there is certainly no way to prove it, so it is just a suggestion—is that somewhere along the jagged line of evolution, our ancestors' brains developed to the point that not only did they have dreams, they also had hallucinations, which they believed were visions. In short, they got smart enough to be fooled by their own brains. There were certainly lots of opportunities for the conditions to exist that could have prompted hallucinations. I'm sure there were times when they were very hungry or thirsty, when they had walked or run for hours on end, when a mushroom or leaf that looked like something they had eaten before but wasn't got mixed into the stew. And so, somewhere along the line, these bigger, more wrinkled brains, functioning a lot better than the brains on previous branches on the tree of humanity, found themselves in a situation where this big brain goes a little haywire and starts rolling a hallucination across the screen of consciousness.

And what do they see in this hallucination? They see what they have seen before as the brain brings back images from memory: places, people, sensations, emotions. And maybe some of those people they see are people who are still alive and maybe some of them are people who are dead.

Now, what do you do with that? You have seen a dead person looking alive and well, and it isn't just a dream because you are awake and it all looks so real. Do you say, "Well, it was just my brain acting up under extreme conditions," or the influence of foreign substances? Not back then you don't. And maybe this happens a few times and somebody figures out how to make it happen, at least sometimes. What do you do with this?

Now, this is admittedly all conjecture, but I suspect one thing somebody came up with is that these hallucinations are really visions, that what they are seeing is a spirit world that is just as real in its own way as this world we live in. That there is something else, something beyond, where some part of what is alive goes after death, at least for a while. And this something, this spirit, can be contacted under certain circumstances. And this spirit probably needs the spirits of the same things it had here, the spirit of food, the spirit of a good hand axe, the spirit of a nice necklace to wear, the spirit of some good clothes.

And so we have religion, the belief in something else, something beyond this life. But if there are spirits of people and animals that live on, are there other spirits? Are there more powerful spirits? Are there spirits in this world as well as the next? Are there spirits of the lightning and thunder, the rain and snow, the sun and moon, the earth and the stars, the plants and animals, the fertility of the soil and of women? Should we call these powerful spirits "gods"? And how can we get on the gods' good side? And now you have theology, the study of the gods.

But that also is not for today. Today, the final question is: If this is really how religion started, with hallucinations that were believed to be visions, what does that mean to us today? Isn't our religion today based on "visions" recorded in scriptures? How should we look at our religion, whatever it is, if at its base is a series of visions? Are visions real? Certainly, Moses and Samuel and Peter and James and John and Paul thought so. Were our deep ancestors right in interpreting what they were seeing as a vision of another reality? Is there another existence out there that we can occasionally glimpse when the two realities touch for some reason?

One thing we have to keep in mind, even if we accept the

possibility of visions being real, is that not all visions are right. History is full of examples of people who either had visions that were wrong or had visions that they interpreted badly or who claimed to have visions when they really didn't in order to get something—power, respect, money, sex, whatever. Paul, our Christian mystic, along with just about every other mystic through time, talks about how to tell a true vision from a false vision. Certainly, groups like the Millerites, who gave away all their stuff and climbed a mountain on a designated day to greet the Second Coming, were following a false vision. Jim Jones's disciples drinking the Kool-Aid in South America were certainly following a false vision. There is no question that not all visions people claim are *true* visions. There are too many false prophets proclaiming false visions, even if they believe those false visions with all their heart, for us to trust those claims without a whole shaker of salt and checking them six ways from Sunday. Far too many have come up short.

But the real question is: Are any visions true? Were Paul and Moses and those primitive ancestors so long ago actually seeing something real, even if it was not of this world? Or were they all seeing hallucinations, not visions? Is our assumption that there is something else, something beyond, no matter how elaborated it has become over the centuries, based on hallucinations, something interpreted as a vision of something real when it was just brainwaves getting jumbled?

Religion is not just a belief in an afterlife. Religion also deals with morality, the nature of humanity, why the universe and nature are what they are. But most religions also believe in something beyond. Certainly, it is comforting to believe there is something beyond, some other reality to which that which is us will go after death, to be with family and friends again, to take our trusty hand axe and cut up our eland steak while sitting around the warm campfire. And if there is some kind of judgment involved, certainly it is better to believe than not and certainly better to be a good person than a bad one, but I think we also have to keep in mind where all this religion started and maybe keep a little question mark in mind when we get too sure of ourselves about all this religion business.

Maybe those far ancestors had a true vision, but it is never a good idea to forget where you came from, and that goes for beliefs as well as people. Under any circumstances, it is a good idea to remember that our religion, any religion, did not spring straight from the mouth of some deity, complete and whole. It grew gradually, at least partly based on a series of visions, changing as knowledge and conditions changed. But it all started tens of thousands of years ago when our ancestors saw something that wasn't there and decided they had glimpsed something beyond.

Amen.

Sermon Two

Purpose

What's religion good for anyway? Today, we might say that it gets us into heaven—if we do it right. But people had religion long before they had any idea of heaven as some kind of paradise you go to when you die or after you get resurrected. People used to think in terms of a spirit world not too different from this one or a Sheol where you were only a shadow in a less-than-pleasant place. So what is religion, in general, good for? In his book, *The World Until Yesterday,* Jared Diamond summarizes the modern scholarship about what functions religion played, and maybe still plays, among people from long ago up through not so long ago. Today, I would like to talk about those functions and see if our modern practice of religion is still fulfilling the same purposes.

The first function is that religion explains things. Somewhere along the line, humans got smart enough to notice that some things cause other things to happen. It's not that things just are; there are causes and effects, at least on the scale we can observe things (let's not get into quantum theory here), and if you can figure these relationships out, then you can explain things, maybe even control them.

Now, some explanations are pretty easy. You stick enough spears in a deer and it dies because the blood, which is life, runs out through the holes the spears made. Plants grow more in the summer because there is more sunshine. But how come the sun comes up every morning? How come flowers in the desert bloom after a rain? How come people from another river valley speak a different language?

Well, for things you don't understand and can't control, one possible explanation is that God did it. Or at least a god of some kind. Maybe the sun comes up because Apollo is pulling it across the sky behind his chariot. Maybe flowers bloom because the rain is the sky god spilling sky god semen on the mother earth goddess. And maybe people speak different languages because in the past human beings got too uppity and tried to build a tower up to heaven and God created a bunch of different languages so people couldn't work together and wouldn't be a threat to him anymore. In short, religion explained things in terms people could understand, even if it wasn't always the best explanation.

Of course, the problem is that as we learned more and more about nature and physics and the universe around us, there was less and less we didn't understand and needed a god as part of the explanation. We now know the sun seems to come up because we live on a big, round planet that is rotating on its axis and orbiting the sun. We now understand the evaporation and condensation cycles of water in the atmosphere and the presence of moisture in the soil as a trigger of plant growth. We have reconstructed the process of language differentiation into dialects, and then separate languages among physically separated groups, and even observed that process in action.

Many of the conflicts we have seen in religion have come when new understandings in science have conflicted with our understandings of God. Evolution is one of the current, classic examples. Evolution is an explanation of how plants and animals and human animals came to be the way we are. It does not depend on God doing any big miracles except maybe way back at the beginning, billions of years ago, being some kind of "first cause"—maybe. Evolution has been repeatedly tested and has passed every test; it has been used to make predictions that in turn proved to be accurate; it is being used as the basis for modifying living things by almost all farmers, animal breeders, and lots of agribusinesses, whether they admit it or even know it. But it also tells us that the stories in Genesis are explanations people came up with thousands of years ago when they had no concept of DNA or molecules or even cells. They're great stories, and they may tell us important things about the relationship between men and gods, but they don't explain how plants or animals or humans actually got started.

But some of us can't seem to let those stories go because we think giving them up as explanations makes God less powerful, less important. It's the same mentality that said the earth had to be the center of the universe because what God made, namely human beings and the place God created for humans to live, namely the earth, had to be the most important thing; hence, the sun must go around the earth, not the earth around the sun. It took a few hundred years, but even the Catholic Church finally admitted Galileo was right and that the earth goes around the sun and the sun is just a minor star out on one of the outer arms of a middling galaxy a long, long way from the center of the universe (assuming the idea of the universe having a center has any meaning).

If God is less powerful because the earth goes around the sun or because human beings and chimpanzees had a common ancestor millions of years ago (which I think may be taking an overly simplistic view of God), then maybe God is going to have to put up with being less powerful. In fact, in almost every case where the common concept of God as an explanation of nature has been found to be logically inconsistent with a developing scientific understanding of nature, eventually, it is the scientific understanding that has prevailed and the concepts of God that had to be modified.

So, back to the point. One of the things religion used to do was explain things in nature and the universe that we couldn't understand. Now, I'm not saying that modern scientific understanding can explain everything in the universe—far from it. Every discovery seems to expose two or three new mysteries: dark matter, dark energy, the imbalance of matter and antimatter, big voids in the distribution of stars. What I am saying is that we no longer look to God as an explanation of these mysteries. This is a function of religion that is no longer viable, and those that try to hang on to it are fighting a losing fight.

Now, that idea will probably cause some anxiety to some of you, which brings us to another function of religion: easing anxiety. This is a dangerous world, and it was even more dangerous way back when. When you know there are dangers, problems that you can't solve or even do anything about, it's normal to get anxious, to worry, to feel like there's nothing you can do. One of the things that religion does is give you something to do. It gives you the feeling that when life is out of control, you can influence something that does have control. Specifically, you can pray or make an offering or perform a ritual or otherwise prompt a god to do something about this mess you find yourself in. If nothing else, that at least reduces your anxiety.

Way back when, people offered prayers and sacrifices and rituals before doing something dangerous, like going hunting or off to fight or going into childbirth. And there were certainly a lot more things to be anxious about back in the hunter-gatherer days—wild animals, floods, droughts, attacks by other tribes, attacks by people in your own tribe, disease, infection, accidents, etc., etc., etc. While hunter-gatherer groups can usually find all the food they need pretty easily once they learn the lay of the land and actually have an easy life most of the time, they have no margin for error. Remember, they can only own what they can carry, so there's no stash of extra food in the house; there's not even a house. One year the berries don't grow or the animal migration route changes and they go hungry for maybe weeks. A stag you're hunting makes an unexpected move and you've got an antler in your guts. Your baby is a breech birth and you both end up dead. If life was at all like some of the hunter-gatherer groups from the last century, your chances of being murdered or otherwise dying violently are about at least one in five or so. There was a lot to be anxious about back then.

Now, some of that started changing once settlements and then farming came along. The story of Joseph in Egypt and the seven fat years and the seven lean years is an example of centralized governments taxing citizens, building up a surplus in storage, and bailing people out when times got tough. Agriculture actually decreased nutrition, and settlements increased disease but made it possible for larger groups to live together, have more children, build permanent shelters from storms, create laws and police, support priests who studied the stars and seasons to predict floods and times to plant. This, at least, decreased anxiety about some things.

Today, well, if you want to see a wild animal dangerous enough to kill you, you probably have to go to a zoo. We still get an occasional flood, but we've got all these dams that make them a lot smaller than they used to be and the National Weather Service usually gives us at least two or three day's warning, just like they warn us about thunderstorms and the possibility of tornadoes. We've seen in the past few years how earthquakes and tsunamis can surprise us and create both awful and awesome death tolls, but tsunami warning buoys are being installed in some oceans right now and the geologists are getting closer and closer to being able to predict earthquakes. And if you go to Charleston, a pretty earthquake-prone place, you'll see the metal circles at regular intervals on the old houses where reinforcements have been installed to keep the houses from collapsing on top of you when there is an earthquake.

The murder rate is just about the lowest in history, as best we can tell. Here in the United States, we lose more people to automobile accidents than to wars, and now in some places more to drug overdoses than to automobile accidents. The point is not that there is nothing to be anxious about but there are a darnsight-fewer dangerous things around that we can't do anything about ourselves than there were way back when. Yes, cancer is scary, but there is lots of medical research going on and we could support even more. Sure, nuclear bombs are scary, but there are groups trying to prevent their use, successfully so far, and even their production. Climate change and environmental problems are scary, but I can recycle and drive a more efficient car and pay a little more to get solar and wind energy up and running. There are very few problems left about which we can do absolutely nothing.

So, while this function of religion to reduce our anxiety about things we can't control is still important, it probably isn't as urgent as it once was. Today, when we recite the Lord's Prayer or pray the rosary or make the sign of the cross, most of us probably aren't really concerned about getting killed today. We might be anxious about getting into college or getting a good job or keeping our marriage together, but those are all things that we can do something about and have some control over and aren't totally dependent on God to help us out.

However, there are, as there always have been, a few things we can't do anything about, which brings us to the next function of religion: providing comfort. We are all going to die. I'm going to die, you're going to die, our parents are going to die, our children are going to die. *We are all going to die.* To make matters worse, life is not always a lot of fun. For most people, for most of history, it's been pretty much stuffed with pain and sorrow. The hunter-gatherers didn't have to deal much with some people having it better than others since they were all pretty much in the same boat, and despite their slim margin for error or disaster, most of the time their life was actually easy compared to farmers and other working stiffs. But as soon as we started keeping herds of domesticated animals or settled down and started farming, some people ended up having it better than others, groups got big enough that you could get away with things, and it soon became obvious that life is not fair.

That, if anything, has only gotten worse as the years have passed. If you have been in this life very long, you soon realize that bad things happen to good people and good things happen to bad people. The entire Book of Job is about the problem of having a good, caring God who is all-powerful, all-knowing, and always present and still having evil exist. And you can argue all day and into the night (and believe me, philosophers and theologians have) about why evil exists. Is there some evil god, almost as powerful as Yahweh? Is it an inevitable corollary to the existence of free will, if free will exists? Is it a test to see who really is faithful or good or believes the right things? Is it just the nature of good that it only exists in comparison to evil, like hot exists only in comparison to cold? Does God just really have a weird sense of humor? At the end of the Book of Job, God basically steps up and says, "I'm God, you're not, so shut up and deal with it," which may be good advice but doesn't really answer the question.

But whatever the answer is, we are stuck with the facts that evil exists and death is coming. And it's at this point that religion says, "Yeah, but it's okay because death is not the end of the game." Whether it's the Vikings in Valhalla and their Ragnarok cycle of world destruction and rebirth, or the Second Coming of Christ and tossing the bad guys into the lake of fire, or the almost endless cycle of reincarnation in Hinduism, one of the big things religion does is make life and death bearable because death is not the final ending.

Okay, so some Nazi war criminals managed to escape and live out peaceful, comfortable lives; they will get their due when they burn forever in hell. So the guy who lied to your boss and got you fired so he could get your job ended up ruining your life, but you wouldn't want to be him when he runs into Saint Peter at the Golden Gate. So your wife cheated on you and then divorced you in order to marry a richer, handsomer man; you think her sexy looks are going to cut her any slack when the angels start sorting the sheep from the goats? So I never smoked but I ended up with cancer, and those rock stars who smoked, drank, and used all kinds of drugs are still playing concerts and attracting the women; I bet the devil is going to tell them what they can do with those guitars once he's their audience. And I'll be sitting in heaven, eating chess pie, listening to Paul Simon music, and hanging around with people who love me. That is the comfort of religion—that sooner or later the scales will balance, that good will eventually win, and that no matter how much we suffer in this life and how inevitable death is, that is not the end.

In the last few decades, there have been movements like

communism and humanism and some others that have put their emphasis on life here on Earth as what is important. They say that there may or not be an afterlife, but what matters is making life here and now as fair and tolerable as possible, that we need to improve life for people here and now, not just promise them "pie in the sky when you die," as Joe Hill put it in one of his pro-union songs back in 1911. There is probably a lot of truth to that.

As some of the other functions of religion have lost value over the years, people have begun to question the nature and even the existence of a soul or a heaven or a resurrection. Frankly, some of their questions are pretty hard to answer. But, as far as I can tell, most people simply do not have the courage to face the idea that this is all there is, that our life and death will have no meaning that exists beyond the memory of us. That is not an idea most people can accept. Life is just too hard and too unfair. We need the comfort of hope that there is something beyond, whether there is or not, wrapped around us like a blanket, holding us like our mother's arms. Otherwise, life is indeed too much for us. So I do not see this function of religion going away anytime soon. This one we still need, though we can't use it as an excuse to not make life better in the here and now.

The next function of religion is actually not as old as the ones we have talked about so far. Hunter-gatherers don't really need much organization or leadership. Everybody pretty much has the same job—men hunt, women gather; you do what needs doing. When your tribe is 150 people max, half of whom are female and many of whom are children, when some decision needs to be made, the twenty or thirty grown men can just sit around and talk it out until everybody pretty much agrees. But once you start settling down and get hundreds, maybe thousands, of people trying to live together, things change.

Now, there are advantages to settling in one place and living in larger groups. You have more warriors to fight off the wandering tribes; you can collect surplus food and store it for later, like Joseph did; you can build things like defensive walls (remember Jericho, which is one of the oldest cities in the history of the world); you can build irrigation ditches and water supply systems (Jerusalem had one of the better water systems around). Eventually, you can put together an army and take over the better farmland or the larger water supply from the other guys and make life better for everybody on your side.

But to do all this good stuff, you need organization and a certain amount of conformity and obedience. Somebody has to be the boss. Those irrigation ditches have to line up and all be pretty much the same size. That army needs somebody to tell people where to line up and when to shoot the arrows. Somebody has to decide how much food everybody chips in during the good years and how much gets doled out during the bad years. Like it or not, when you have a lot of people living together, you have to have at least some government, some taxes, some laws, somebody in charge. And those people don't have time to gather their own food; they have to be fed from what everybody else grows.

So, how do you get everybody to go along with this new way of living, this organization with rules and bureaucrats? The answer all the early settlers came up with was the same: the boss is a god. The king or chief or whatever the top guy was called was either a god (like Pharaoh), or was picked by God (like Saul and David), or could become a god (like the Caesars in Rome), or at least had some kind of direct link to god. So good harvests and timely rain from the gods depended on the king doing the religious stuff, the prayers and rituals, in a way that pleased the gods, which meant he needed priests to advise and guide him and make sure everybody else followed the religion. Of course, he also needed soldiers to protect his kingdom and his subjects, which meant he also needed tax collectors to gather both the surpluses and the food to support the king and his court and his priests and his army. And, of course, all this only worked if everybody pretty much believed the same religion, especially the part about the king having an in with the gods.

So, those good old priests had to promote basically a uniform religion, the same basic beliefs about the gods, taught to the people by using the same rituals, praying the same prayers, singing the same hymns all over the kingdom. And all those religions pretty much said you had to do what the king and his government told you to do because he spoke with the voice of god and loved and cared for his people and only wanted what was best for them, even if that meant you had to cough up an extra bushel of grain this year and spend a month working on some public works project, like a pyramid or a temple.

So basically, government started out claiming religion and government were one and the same. The king was divinely ordained by God or the gods and was the head of both the church and the state. And the function of religion was to promote all this organization and standardization and conformity and obedience that were necessary for large groups of people who weren't related to live together.

And it sort of worked for a long time. Egyptian dynasties lasted a long time. Rome's civic religion enabled it to build an empire. The Catholic Church's physical empire has recently shrunk down to Vatican City, but there were Papal States in Italy for hundreds of years.

But it turns out there are two problems with using religion to prop up a government. The first is, if you are fighting for a king who is a god or has a god on his side and you lose, what does that say about your god? If your king turns out to be a sniveling idiot, what does that say about your god? If your king takes so much of your food that you starve, what does that say about your god? Tying religion to government generally turns out to be bad for the religion.

Now, the Greeks and the Romans were pretty good at looking at the religions of the people they had defeated and saying, "Okay, your god of the sky looks a lot like our god of the sky; it's probably the same god, just going by different names, so let's throw a lamb on the alter together and have a drink." But those monotheistic religions just somehow couldn't be quite as tolerant. We Christians, as well as the Jews and Muslims, have a bad record of saying it's our way or the highway, which brings us to the second problem with mixing government and religion.

This second problem, of course, is that it requires everybody in the country to pretty much believe the same religion. Theological disagreements are tantamount to treason and political disagreements become spouting heresies. Look at what the Catholics did to the Huguenots in France. Anybody remember Bloody Mary, Queen of England? Henry VIII had to start a whole new religion to get a divorce, and his kids Edward, Mary, and Elizabeth had to deal with a whole lot of rebellion on opposite sides before the dust settled. Not to mention all the Crusades, the Troubles in Ireland, and thousands of other religious wars through the centuries. Not to mention that the United States was partly founded by people trying to get away from a state religion.

It took us a while, but I like to think we have finally figured out that promoting government by using religion or religion by using government is generally a bad idea these days, especially for the religion. I know there are people running around now saying the United States is a "Christian" nation, but I hope they are wrong. I don't think we want to be a Christian nation. What are we going to do, kick out all the Jews, Muslims, Buddhists, Hindus, Bahá'ís, atheists, agnostics, Wiccans, Confucians, Shintos, and Animists? Do the Baptists then fight the Catholics? If the Baptists win, do they turn on the Presbyterians? There's an old joke among the Baptists that the reason there are so many little Baptist churches is that whenever one member of a church couldn't agree with another member about something, one of them would leave and start a new church. How does that work if one church controls the police department and the other church controls the highway patrol? No, I think—I hope—that the separation of church and state is an idea that will grow, making this particular function of religion, of promoting government and obedience to rulers, obsolete.

Another function of religion that wasn't much needed long, long ago is codes of how to treat strangers. When you lived in a little tribe of around one hundred people, most of whom you were related to one way or another, anybody you didn't know was an enemy—period, stop, end. Right and wrong and morality were not major issues because your behavior toward others was determined by your relationship: close family you had certain obligations to, relatives by marriage a different set of obligations, the rest of your clan a different set, and the rest of the tribe one final set of relationships and obligations. Anybody else might not even be considered human, but certainly worth killing.

This version of morality tends not to work when you try to live with people you are not related to. And one of the functions of religion was to provide rules and customs for how to get along with all these strange people. Before, murdering a stranger was considered a good thing. Now, maybe not so much. And it was religion that laid out the new rules of right and wrong and good and bad, and used the power of access to the gods to persuade people to go along, and the power of the king or chief and their henchmen to enforce these new rules.

Look at the Ten Commandments and the other laws in the Books of the Law. Look at the even earlier Code of Hammurabi. God and his king or priests are laying down the rules of how to get along with people you aren't related to and maybe even have never met before. They are rules everybody has to follow because everybody will be better off if everybody follows these rules. And if you don't, God will get you, even if he uses one of the king's officers to do it.

Now, we still need all those rules and laws about getting along with strangers today, all those "do not murder," "do not steal," "do not rape" rules, as well as "don't pass on the right," "do stop for school buses," and "don't spit on the sidewalk." The question is, do we need God-playing policeman to back them up? Again, what worked years ago when everybody was the same religion doesn't necessarily work now when there are many religions all trying to live together. Conflicts pop up when we can't tell the difference between a law that is promoting good behavior no matter what your religion and a law promoting a ritual or belief of a specific religion. Not all religions believe homosexuality is evil. As Christians, we don't want Jews telling us what we can and cannot eat, nor Muslims telling us how many times a day to pray. If we don't want to be constantly fighting wars, we have to realize we can't use the force of law to put crosses on courthouse lawns, close businesses on Sundays, or determine who can buy a wedding cake. You want prayer in schools? Fine, let's line up the prayers to Allah, the Great Spirit, Shiva, and Mother Earth, etc. and make sure everybody gets their shot. That's only fair, right?

The purpose is to find ways to live in the same nation, state, city, and neighborhood. We have to figure out what's really going to be good for everybody, not what's good for just us. It's not good for anybody to allow people to drive ninety miles an hour down the highway. It's not good for anybody to allow cheating in the stock market. Allowing murder, theft, abuse, assault, fraud, even shoplifting or jaywalking is not good for anybody in the long run. If we think about it, these are rules we need to live together, and we are all much better off if we follow them and pay taxes to hire police to make sure we all follow them. It's in our own self-interest. But it hurts us all if we mix that self-interest up with religion. So, again, we need to think twice and three times before we ask the government to enforce something that is religious. It usually makes the religion look bad and even be resented and opposed by those who follow even a slightly different religion or denomination. The time for this function of religion has passed.

The last function of religion is also one that developed only after we moved past the hunter-gatherer culture, and that function is justifying war. Hunter-gatherers actually go to war a lot, competing for water and good hunting or gathering grounds, but they don't need religion to justify it since everybody outside your tribe or kin group is automatically an enemy. It's only when you settle down in towns and cities that you have to have those "thou shalt not kill" commandments from on high to keep the group together for the entire group's benefit. But then it gets confusing if it's not okay to kill this group of strangers, but it's a good thing to kill that group of strangers.

God sent the Ten Commandments down the mountain, saying, "Thou shalt not murder," but once they got into the Promised Land, the order was to commit genocide left and right. In fact, the

Israelites frequently got dressed down by God because they didn't kill all the women and children in the towns they conquered. So, "thou shalt not kill" only meant "don't kill other people of your religion, but wipe out anybody of another religion." It's your religious duty to kill the heathens. So, you not only get the whole history of religious wars, some of which we have already mentioned, but you also get the various kings and emperors wanting to get a bigger empire, crying, "For God and country," "Kill the idolaters," "By the sign of the cross, we conquer."

Sad to say, there have also been plenty of "missionaries" who felt the locals were not converting from their heathen faith fast enough and were even resisting the pious missionary efforts, who were not hesitant to call in the army to teach these primitives a thing or two about resisting the true faith.

Reading the histories of Christians in the New World, sometimes one wonders if they saved more than they killed. And again, sadly, this kind of thinking is not all in the past. Certainly, we have seen some of the radical Islamists consider us as heathens outside the true faith and therefore fair game for killing, and some so-called Christians saying in turn that all Muslims need to be kicked out or otherwise dealt with as people who are not part of our fellowship of true believers, and hence not really entitled to as much right to live as we have.

It doesn't take much imagination to see where that kind of thinking leads in a world as interconnected and intermingled as we are now. National defense is one thing; holy crusades are another. Holy wars tend to get out of hand and be exceedingly cruel because, after all, you are fighting for your god, and the other guy is a heathen heretic who wants to destroy your religion as well as your county and really isn't as fully human as you are. I would like to hope that when we fight wars in the future, as I'm sure we will, that we will be at least honest with ourselves and know that we are fighting for power, or resources, or water, or economic advantage, or freedom, or self-defense, or whatever, and leave God out of it. There may or may not be such a thing as a "just war," but there is no "just, holy war." I would like to believe that God has gotten out of the genocide business, and we should too.

Those are the functions of religion that Jared Diamond summarized about human life from the beginning up until modern day, but there is one more function that Diamond talks about when he writes about "badges of commitment," which is what he calls the various activities or appearances that identify a person as belonging to a particular religious group. Basically, religion creates a community—a larger form of extended family, people to whom we are related not by blood or DNA but by common beliefs, rituals, practices, and behaviors.

Back in the day, community was automatic. You had your family, your clan, and your tribe. No hunter-gatherer had to wonder who was in his community and who wasn't. Today, it's not so easy. Sure, we're all Americans or whatever, but our families are scattered all over the place, held together by cell phone and video calls. Clans and tribes have pretty much faded away, replaced by churches, fraternal organizations, and social groups. We're Presbyterians, Masons and Shriners, VFW, UAW, PEO, Delta Delta Delta, Chattahoochee Evening Stars, and Atlanta Driving Club. We create our own clans and tribes, our own communities. But are religions any better at creating communities, or do they create better communities than any of these other groups?

Communities are supposed to be composed of people we can trust, who can be motivated to work together for some common good, who can function in many ways like an extended family by providing emotional, social, and even financial support in times of need. Christianity got a big boost in Rome when a plague came and it was the Christians who stayed and took care of each other when people got sick. We assume we can trust and depend on the people in our religious community—in our case, our church.

The badges of commitment Diamond talks about are what we use to determine who is really in our community and who is just along for the ride, for what they can get out of it. Believe me, I have been in churches long enough to know there are members I wouldn't trust farther than I could throw them, and I'm really bad at throwing people. I grew up as a preacher's kid, and both as a kid and an adult I have known churches and church members to do some really terrible things. So I have no illusions that everybody who wears the T-shirt really plays on the team.

So, how do you tell who is really a member of the real community, who you can trust and turn to for help when needed, who can become a member of your religious family? The answer seems to be that these badges of commitment to the religious group have a cost; they require something not easy to give. At various times in history, this has meant scarring your body or cutting off pieces. It has meant joining "mystery cults" that require expensive or dangerous or painful initiations. It has meant sacrificing expensive animals, giving your last two mites, allowing others to laugh at you for your ridiculous beliefs or rituals. More recently it has meant memorizing large amounts of some holy text, making a pilgrimage to Mecca or Lourdes or Canterbury, or tithing ten percent of your total income before taxes. It used to mean going to Sunday School, Worship Service, Sunday Night Service, Wednesday Prayer Service, and either the

Men's Breakfast or the Women's Circle meetings. Today, I guess it means Confirmation or new member classes and an occasional Worship Service.

But, you see, if the costs of being in the community get too low, being in the community doesn't mean anything anymore. It's not that church becomes just a social group; it's that it doesn't become a *good* social group, a community, an extended family. Look at the religions that are growing, like the Mormons. Being a Mormon—a real Mormon—requires both a lot of time and money: tithing, serving in the church, going on mission trips at your own expense for a year or two. This is not an easy religion to be a part of. Even though it was created by an admitted con man and its scriptures are almost demonstrably a sham, it has survived several attempts to exterminate it and is growing by leaps and bounds because it creates a community among its members. The same can probably be said about the evangelicals, whose scriptural fundamentalism is so full of inherent contradictions that it borders on illogical but who create community with their Sunday schools, small group dinners, conformity, and appeal to fear.

There are dangers to this, of course. Any community that feels that other communities are not as valid or worthwhile or religious as they are is just setting itself up for conflict with other communities. And a community that is too closed, that is too hard to get into, or only accepts people who are born into the community or meet some other biological or ethnic requirement is just cutting its own throat in the long run. But if we look back at all the functions of religion—explaining nature, defusing anxiety, providing comfort, promoting organization, preaching political obedience, developing moral codes, justifying laws, and creating community—it is only providing comfort and creating community that seems to have a long-term future as being central to religion, if religion has a future. Maybe that is something to keep in mind the next time we ask ourselves what our church should do.

Amen.

Sermon Three

Abortion

Today, I want to discuss one of the major ethical issues of our time: Abortion.

Please note that I say "of our time," because it has not always been an issue. In many times and places, especially among nomadic groups, abortion was simply what you did if you became pregnant again too soon after having a child for the simple reason that it was almost physically impossible to feed and carry two babes in arms at the same time while walking from place to place. The only problem was how to have an abortion without killing yourself. Other societies dealt with the problem of ill-timed or unwanted children by killing them or leaving them out on a hillside or something similar, which is technically not abortion but achieves the same end. So, abortion is an issue only among settled societies, especially more modern ones that have developed low-risk means of abortion.

But acknowledging that abortion is a modern issue does not make it less of an issue for us. It simply invalidates those who claim that abortion at all stages of pregnancy has always been considered illegal and a grave sin, which, if you look at things like the law in early America or the pronouncements of the Medieval Catholic Church, simply isn't true. More on that later.

However, I don't think contrasting the laws of the Puritans in Massachusetts in 1650 with the laws in Texas in 2023 is really going to get us anywhere. I think that the real question you have to answer before deciding when abortion is right or wrong is: *When does someone become a living human being?* Now, that's really a two-part question, but let's start with the first part: *When do we become alive?*

Now, if you are a fundamentalist (someone who interprets the Bible literally), abortion is not a problem for you because you know a person is not really alive until they take their first breath. The Bible is actually pretty clear on this. Right from the beginning, in Genesis 2:7, it says, "Then the Lord God formed a man from the dust of the ground and breathed into his nostrils the breath of life. Thus the man became a living creature." Later, during Ezekiel's vision of the Valley of the Bones, in chapter 37, the bones have come together, and flesh and skin has been put upon them, but, it says, "there was no breath in them." So, Ezekiel had to prophesy unto the wind, saying, "These are the words of the Lord God: Come, Oh wind, come from every quarter and breathe into these slain, that they may come to life." And only then do the bodies come to life: when they have breath blown into them. Even in the New Testament, in Mark 15:37, when Jesus dies on the cross, Mark says he—to use the King James Version—"gave up the ghost," but that word that was translated as "ghost," according to modern translations, literally means "breath." Jesus gave up the breath.

There are other examples, but it's pretty obvious (if you take the Bible literally) that you are only alive when you are breathing, so a baby is not really alive until it takes its first breath. So, for you fundamentalists out there, abortion is not a problem because you are not killing something that is alive.

However, maybe you are one of those liberal theologians who say, "Wait a minute, you can't always take the Bible literally." You say you have to take into account the historical context, the understanding of science that existed back then, the findings of modern science, the goal of the biblical writer and the target audience, the often poetic literary traditions of the culture, the common use of symbol and metaphor, the cultural beliefs and assumptions of the times, and dozens of other factors, including the way the language itself changed over time, in order to really interpret and understand the scriptures. Then you can say that this was simply the primitive understanding of life thousands of years ago. You can say that, back then, they thought there was something in breath that gave life, that emotions were centered in the heart, and that the earth was flat and rested on the back of a turtle. They didn't know about brain waves and nerve systems or the stages of fetal development.

First of all, I think you're wrong about that last one. People who went out and butchered a sheep or a goat when they needed a big meal had probably figured out the basic processes of pregnancy by now, but I think I get the point. Even if you believe that the Bible is God's Word, you have to take into account that it was written down at certain times and places by certain people using the language they had at that time and place to express ideas according to the customs and concepts of the time in order to communicate to specific groups of people at that time. They were not writing direction manuals in English for people living here and now, so we have to use a little common sense in trying to understand what they were trying to say.

So when, in this modern day and age, do we say something is alive? Surprisingly, that still gets a little tricky. People toss out criteria like something is alive if it can move, it can grow, it can reproduce. What about a virus? Is it alive? It can move, but it doesn't really get bigger. It can't make more viruses by itself; it has to sneak into a cell and hijack the cell's reproductive machinery to get the cell to make more viruses. Is that being alive or just a bunch of complex chemicals all hung together with bioelectrical bonds? We say that the proteins our body makes aren't alive by themselves, but our bodies are basically made of proteins, and we like to think we're alive. So you say, "Enough, let's look up from the electron microscope and get back to people. We're only talking about aborting human embryos and fetuses, not microscopic organisms or even animals."

Which brings us to the second part of the question: *What is a human being?* What makes us different from any other animal? Why do we say these animals fit under one set of rules and human beings fit under another set of rules? Certainly, we are animals. Our DNA works the same way and only varies from a chimpanzee by about 1.6 percent. We breathe the same way; digest the same way; see, hear, smell, touch, and taste using the same kinds of biological mechanisms. Students learn human anatomy by dissecting pigs. We test our drugs on various monkeys and apes; even take some animal parts—for example, pig heart valves—and stick them in our own bodies to fix defective human parts. *We are animals.*

"Yes," you reply, "but we are different: we build things using tools, we have language to communicate with, we create art." At least that's what people used to say made us different. We were the only animals that used tools and language and made art. Well, turns out that's not true either. Turns out lots of animals use tools. Apes will strip the leaves off a branch so they can stick it into a termite mound to pull out termites to eat. Some monkeys use stones to crack open nuts. Even crows have been known to use a little stick to open a latch. We're not the only animal to use tools; we just use them more and better.

Same thing with language. Dolphins have language; they

even have what we think are names for each other. Cats have one set of sounds they use with humans and another set of sounds they only use with other cats. Isn't that a kind of language? Even prairie dogs have different sounds to warn for snakes and eagles so they know whether to look up or down for a threat. We just have more sounds we can make and bigger vocabularies. As for art, have you ever seen a bowerbird nest?

The point is that what we have here is what a logician would call a difference in degree, not in kind. We're not the only animals who make tools or use language or make art; we just use more sophisticated tools, more complex language, and more varied art. So is that the only difference between human beings and other animals? It's at this point that some theologians should speak up and say that what makes us different is that human beings have souls. And that opens a "whole 'nother can of worms."

You see, while I suspect most of you would say you have a soul, that's not really a Christian concept. We have to start really watching our words here, especially the difference between "soul" and "spirit." Back in the Old Testament, most of the people living in the Fertile Crescent, including the Hebrews, believed that if there was something after death, it was in what they called "Sheol." Job put it pretty plainly in chapter 7 when he says, in Robert Alter's translation, "Thus, who goes down to Sheol will not come up. He will not return to his home. His place will not know him again." Later, at the end of chapter 10, Job describes Sheol as "the land of dark and death's shadow, the land of gloom, thickest murk, death's shadow and disorder, where it shines thickest murk." So, Sheol is a place of darkness where people have become "shades," or shadows or images, entities without a body, without personality or strength, knowledge or wisdom, without memory of life. And notice that this is not a punishment. All the dead go to Sheol, both the good and the bad. And from Sheol, there was no return.

So, this is what we find in the Old Testament until we get to the things written during and after the Exile period, such as the Book of Daniel and sections of Isaiah. In Babylon, the Jews were exposed to Zoroastrianism, the most common religion in that section of the world until it was exterminated by Islam hundreds of years later. We're not very familiar with it now since it's pretty much dead, but it had lots of concepts that appear in later Judaism and Christianity, such as the battle between light and dark and the resurrection of the dead. But this was not the resurrection of a soul; it was a resurrection of the body. Isaiah 26 puts it this way: "But thy dead live, their bodies will rise again. They that sleep in the earth will awake and shout for joy; for thy dew is a dew of sparking light, and the earth will bring those long dead to birth again." For Judaism, this is a new idea. This idea is developed again in Daniel, which says in chapter 12, "Many of those that sleep in the dust of the earth will wake, some to everlasting life and some to the reproach of eternal abhorrence,"

Daniel is an interesting book in lots of ways. The story is set during the exile, but the book was actually written later, during the Maccabean period, after Alexander the Great swept through and brought his Macedonian Greek culture with him. Daniel also has some of the earliest apocalyptic literature in the Bible—in the second part of the book after the fiery furnace and the lion's den stories are over. Basically, the situation is that the Macedonian rulers are killing and torturing bunches of Jews for trying to keep the Jewish religious laws and practice the rituals instead of going along with the obviously more civilized Greek ways. If you look in the Apocrypha, you'll see it makes waterboarding look like a kindergarten game.

But the big difference from previous conflicts is that now Jews are being killed for their religion instead of it being just one ethnic group against another for land or access to water, with religion not being that much of a sore spot. So, all these Jews are being executed for their faith, usually pretty painfully, and it brings up a theological question: How can God allow these priests and others to die young and in pain and go down to Sheol forever just because they were faithful to the Law of God? And some people answer this question by saying it isn't forever; God will resurrect them and give them a great reward for their faithfulness by taking them up to a paradise in heaven and sending the bad guys to a Sheol now called, in Greek, Hades.

Now, this idea didn't take off like gangbusters. In fact, even in the New Testament period, it may not have been the majority opinion. Matthew 22:23 says that the Sadducees, who were the conservatives of the day, didn't believe in a resurrection. The book of Mark says the same thing and probably said it first, but whoever wrote Matthew seems to have been a little more up to speed on Jewish issues. Anyway, the implication is that the Pharisees, on the other hand, did believe in a resurrection of some kind. As an aside, the Pharisees, for all the bad rap they get in the New Testament, were the liberals and reformers of the day and were the ones who formed the core of Rabbinical Judaism after the destruction of the Temple, which is probably part of the reason they get so much criticism in the New Testament. The Sadducees were out of power and almost long gone by the time most of the New Testament got written and so weren't a problem for the Christians.

But back to the point. This idea of a resurrection of the body was floating around in religious circles while Jesus was walking around Galilee. But it doesn't really require any kind of soul to exist either after or before death. There may be some "spirit" or "breath" animating life while you're alive, but it's not really necessary for a resurrection since it's your body that will be resurrected.

Compare this with one of the other ideas floating around—an import from the Greeks, called a "soul." The Greek philosophers actually had a lot of arguments about the nature of the soul, but the basic idea was that it was what gave life to the body but could exist without the body. Drawing on the teachings of Socrates, Plato considered the soul to be the essence of a person, the thing that decides how we behave. He considered this essence to be an incorporeal, nonphysical, eternal occupant of our being. Socrates says that even after death, the soul exists and is able to think. He believed that as bodies die, the soul is continually reborn in subsequent bodies, and Plato believed this as well.

Now, this idea of a soul, in all the various philosophical nitpicking, probably goes back even before the Greeks. I guess there's no way to really prove it, but it might go back at least as far as the Indo-Europeans running around the steppes north of the Black and Caspian Seas, since one branch of that group moved southwest and became the Greeks while another branch headed southeast and took over most of northern India. Those who went to India wrote in Sanskrit, and eventually developed Hinduism, which is based on this idea of an immortal soul, which is reincarnated over and over again in an endless wheel of life, moving up or down in castes (or even into animals) depending on the balance of good and bad karma you have accrued by the end of your life. The goal is to keep moving up, life after life, until you eventually gain a true understanding that this life is just an illusion to the point that you can deny yourself and earn only good karma and have your soul merge into Nirvana, the dissolution of self into a nothingness that is unaware of any separateness and finally breaks the wheel of pain and suffering that is life.

So, the point is that this idea of a soul, something that gives life to a body, that exists possibly before and certainly after life, that thinks and reasons and feels and remembers and may go to an afterlife or be reincarnated again and again, is not a new idea; it's just not a Christian idea.

Even though this idea of a soul was known to the New Testament writers, the New Testament comes down pretty firmly on the side of resurrection of the body, not the soul. All the scriptures about people asked to stick fingers in Jesus's side after his resurrection, about him eating fish, about people recognizing him, are intended to make the point that his body has been resurrected, not some ghost or spirit or soul—his body. It might be what the theologians call a "glorified" body, meaning it can get through locked doors and, evidently, isn't feeling any pain from nails or spear points and some other fun stuff, but it is definitely a physical body not so different from what he was before he died. And Paul makes clear, over and over again, that it is a resurrection like Jesus's resurrection that he believes we have to look forward to. Even in Revelation, it's bodies rising from graves to meet Jesus in the sky, not some disembodied essence of a person.

We should now pause a moment to think about what that means to us and how we should think of our bodies. It is our bodies that are going to be resurrected. These physical, sexual, sensual bodies (we hope with some of the aches and pains fixed) are going to be what we will have for eternity, according to the Bible. These bodies are what God loves and what will be with God in heaven, whatever that means. If God loves these bodies that much, maybe we ought to think a little better of them ourselves.

Anyway, back to the main point. Those Greek or Indo-European ideas about souls got all mixed up with Christianity later when people tried to fit Christianity and Greek philosophy together and they got all jumbled up to the point that, today, most people who call themselves Christian believe they have a soul, even though that is certainly not biblical. It also doesn't help the argument that human beings are different from animals because human beings have souls, especially when you consider that both the Greeks and the Hindus thought that animals and maybe even plants had souls. So, if we are trying to decide something about abortion based on whether people have souls, I think we may have to decide first just how much of a Neo-Platonist Christian we are.

There is also another factor to take into account if we say that human beings have souls or something else that enters or arises at conception: People who study conception and pregnancy estimate that at least half, if not more, of all conceptions end in spontaneous abortion, many before the woman even realizes she is pregnant. Just because sperm and ovum get together doesn't mean that every little embryo is going to make it into the world. Now, you can call this "nature dealing with its mistakes" or "God being the biggest abortionist in the universe," but if there is something like a soul that enters the fertilized cell at conception, then most of the souls ever conceived never get to be born. Are there really billions and billions of conceived but unborn souls floating around in some ethereal netherworld? Or do they just get reincarnated in the next available fertilized cell until they finally land in one that gets born? Frankly, I think that kind of idea is too full of logical inconstancies to take much further.

So, where are we? We don't really know when something is alive, and we really don't know what makes a human being different from any other animal except we're smart enough to ask if anything makes us different from other animals. So, what do we do about abortion?

Well, one thing we can do is ask what others have said about abortion and when life starts. The Supreme Court once said, basically, that a fetus is not legally a living human being until it is "viable"—that is, able to live even if it is born early. In early America, most laws said what happened to a fetus was up to the mother until the "quickening," the time when the mother can feel the fetus moving inside her womb. Until then, the mother could do pretty much whatever she wanted to about her pregnancy, depending on how big a risk she wanted to take with whatever form of abortion was available to her. This was basically the accepted law in most of the United States well into the 1800s, when the doctors began opposing any abortions not done by doctors as unsafe or unsanitary.

Today, people talk about when there is an identifiable heartbeat or active brainwaves or avoidance of pain or evidence of consciousness, though how you measure that is not totally clear. Even the Catholic Church has changed its thinking over time. Aquinas, following that great Christian theologian Aristotle, said a fetus didn't have a soul, thus was not alive, until it was forty days old for a male and eighty days old for a female (females being the result of defective seed). Thus abortion was wrong before these dates, but it wasn't killing a human being and deserved a lesser punishment. Pope Gregory XIII agreed with the forty-day limit, Sextus VI, his successor, said that was rubbish and any abortion was homicide. The next Pope, Gregory XIV, said just to ignore most of what Sextus said. In the 600s, the Irish Catholic Church put the penalty for abortion at three and a half years of penitence, but the penalty for having illicit sex was seven and a half years on bread and water. In 1140, church law said abortion was homicide only after the fetus was "formed," whatever that meant. It wasn't until 1869 that Pius IX officially declared all abortion was homicide, and that ruling was later incorporated into Canon Law in 1917.

Again, the point is that this is not a question with an obvious or even consistent answer. Neither life nor humanity are easy to draw a line around but seem to have very fuzzy edges. Trying to fit the idea of a soul into the theology of a resurrection of the body or the basic facts of biology just seems to lead to contradictions. So, what do we do? Where do we go from here?

I would like to make two suggestions: First, that we all admit this is a problem to which there is no good answer. Life is complex—bad things happen to good people; situations arise when the right thing to do is not obvious. Sometimes there is no right thing, only more or less bad things. And we are all very poor at predicting the outcome of our decisions. Does an abortion kill the potential next Einstein, or the lack of an abortion condemn a potential Madam Curie to a life of poverty and ignorance? We are not God, and we cannot know. There is nothing in this life as dangerous as a person who is absolutely sure what is right, and I can almost guarantee you that person is wrong.

Second, I would like to suggest that any hard and fast rule, law, doctrine, or statement of ethics that anyone could come up with that was universally applied to abortion would be wrong at least some of the time. We have seen how the edict that the soul enters at conception and killing a living soul is wrong has led to the cruel deaths of women with medical problems that could be solved by an abortion. So, we end up with dead mothers and either dead or motherless babies instead of one aborted fetus. This is not Christian love; this is insanity.

"But there has to be some limit," you say. "Otherwise, we could have women demanding abortions a week before the baby is due to be born. There has to be some rule, some law." But that is just the point. No law, secular or canon, can really cover all the circumstances. Technology keeps pushing back how early in development a fetus could be saved at the same time it is getting better and better at detecting physical and genetic defects and potential complications. Each case is different—rape, incest, abusive parents, medical complications, genetic birth defects, extreme poverty, extreme youth, mental problems, abusive spouses or lovers, exposure to drugs or toxins, community or religious attitudes—hundreds and hundreds of complications and factors have to be taken into account. No Congress or synod has that kind of wisdom.

We can preach principles, we can promote morality and can provide protection, but we cannot legislate a solution to this problem without creating cruelty and evil in the application of our laws to some of the cases. We might suggest some guidelines, but no hard and fast rule will ever work all the time. Even well-meaning attempts to help often have cruel side effects.

Well into the 1950s, pregnant unmarried girls in places like Ireland were often shipped off to convents and put to work doing laundry and scrubbing floors until their babies were born, then the babies were ripped away from them a few days later and put up for adoption God knows where. Even today there are old men and women begging to know who their birth mother was and getting only silence. This is not a problem with good solutions, only bad choices.

So, if there are no good rules, only a few basic principles like love, respect, the value of life, forgiveness, and compassion, what do we do? How do we value one bad choice against another bad choice? How do we decide?

And I tell you, "we" don't. It's not our decision to make. We can preach and proclaim, model behavior and provide guidance, support and offer alternatives, try to prevent and protect, but we cannot decide. We cannot repent of someone else's sins, we cannot believe in someone else's place, and we cannot decide about someone else's life. Only the person standing before God can decide. Otherwise, we play God and end up doing evil. It is the woman with the embryo in her womb that must decide. She is the only one with that awful and awe-filled responsibility. And God help her.

Amen.

Sermon Four

Homosexuality

This time I want to talk about another controversial subject in our community: homosexuality. So, if there are any of you who want to send your children out, I guess this is the time. However, I urge you to let your teenagers stay for two reasons: First, so they can hear sex talked about politely, using the proper terms. Second, so they can explain some of those terms to you when you get home. (Sorry, cheap joke.)

Being good Christians, we'll start out by looking at what Jesus said about homosexuality. Turning to the Gospel of . . . Oh, well maybe in . . . No, then over in . . . Nope, sorry, Jesus never said anything about homosexuality, for or against. But we all know the Bible must be against it somewhere, so let's go back to the Old Testament and look in the Books of the Law. Ah, here it is, Leviticus 18:22: "And with a male you shall not lie as one lies with a woman. It is an abhorrence." And similarly in Leviticus 20:13: "And a man who lies with a male as one lies with a woman, the two of them have done an abhorrent thing. They are doomed to die. Their bloodguilt is upon them." That seems pretty plain. But just to be sure, let's be good biblical scholars and look at the context, the other verses around these. By the way, I'm using the Robert Alter translation when possible because it comes with such great footnotes.

Leviticus is a book of laws. Most of the laws relate to how to carry out the sacrifices and how to religiously purify people, places, and things. This is where the rules about what you can and cannot eat (the kosher rules) come from. It is about the practices and behaviors that are to set the Jews apart from the rest of the world, create a separate community distinct from their closely related neighbors, and keep them pure before God. Chapter 17 is about not drinking blood or eating animals that died naturally or were killed by predators. Chapter 19 has a wide variety of rules, including elaborations on some of the Ten Commandments, like the famous ones about honoring your mother and father and loving your fellow man like you love yourself. But it also has laws against eating sacrificed meat more than two days old, reaping all the grain or picking all the fruit without leaving some for the poor, not paying workers promptly, making jokes about the deaf, planting two kinds of grain in the same field, wearing clothes made of two kinds of fabric, getting a tattoo, or summoning ghosts.

Chapter 21 has laws that apply to the sons of Aaron, the priests, who aren't to touch dead bodies except their own close kin or shave their heads or trim their beards. They also can't marry a divorced woman or a widow, not to mention a prostitute. For that matter, a man can't become a priest if he has a physical disability, is blind, is hunchback or a dwarf, has a skin problem, or even a broken leg or arm.

And among all these laws and regulations, chapters 18 and 20 list who you cannot have sex with. A man can't have sex with his mother, his father's other wives (if his father has more than one), his own sister or half sister, his granddaughter, his stepmother's daughter, his aunt, his daughter-in-law, or his sister-in-law. A man also can't have sex with both a woman and her daughter or a woman and her granddaughter, or both a woman and her sister unless the woman dies first. He can't have sex with a woman during her menstrual period, or with another man's wife.

Child sacrifice is definitely a no-no. Bestiality is also out for men and women. And a man can't lie with a man "as one lies with a woman," which one of Alter's fabulous footnotes explains means anal or intercrural intercourse, "intercrural" meaning, of course, between the crura, which, as everyone knows, are parts of the legs.

Chapter 20 repeats some of the same prohibitions for the man, adding punishments. Child sacrifice gets the death penalty, as does adultery (but not fornication). Vilifying or insulting your parents gets the death penalty, but calling up ghosts and spirits just gets exile. Having sex with one of your father's wives or your daughter-in-law gets death for both unless the woman is forced. Having sex with a mother and her daughter gets all three of you burned to death. Bestiality's punishment of death goes for both the man or woman and the animal. Having sex with your sister or half sister or with a woman during her period gets exile for both people unless the woman is forced. Somehow, God will make men who have sex with their aunt or sister-in-law barren. And a man who lies with a male as with a woman is doomed to die, though again, one of Alter's footnotes clarifies that the Talmud interprets this as anal penetration.

The footnotes also point out the importance of three things that are not said: First of all, female homosexuality is not mentioned at all. This seems to be because lesbian activity does not involve the wasting of semen. What happens to semen seems to have been a big deal back then. The tipoff on this may be the word they used for semen, "seed." People back then didn't really know about DNA and chromosomes or cell division. They did know about planting seeds in Mother Earth and having plants

49

grow and about breeding sheep and other animals. That's how they stayed alive and even got rich. So, the analogy they drew was between planting a seed in the earth and the male planting his seed in the female's womb, whether that was a sheep or a human.

The idea was that the seed contained all that was alive, and the earth or womb provided the fertile ground that the seed needed to germinate and grow. So, a man's semen contained these little seeds with, if not a teeny-tiny person, at least the essence of what would become a person. A seed was alive, it was precious, not to be wasted by putting it somewhere it wouldn't be able to grow. That would be almost like killing all these little potential babies. But lesbian sex, since nobody was wasting any semen, evidently wasn't a concern to God. Which in some ways, makes the second omission even more puzzling.

All of the references to male homosexuality are specific to anal sex or something very close to it. Believe me, manual and oral sex were not unknown to these people. Check out some of the old art that they don't put in the history books or some of the old stories that were never intended to be part of any Bible. But these other forms of potential homosexual activity do not seem to be, as Alter put it, "of urgent concern." Perhaps this is because these activities were not as similar to heterosexual intercourse—only with a male taking the female role—because taking the other sex's role was part of the problem. After all, women were lesser creatures, so a man doing something feminine was disgraceful. And being the receptive partner in a sexual act was definitely feminine. Or maybe they just expected that the prohibition was to be understood to extend to those activities, perhaps because they didn't want to talk about such delicate subjects even in the law. It's one of those things in the Bible, or in this case *not* in the Bible, that nobody has been able to satisfactorily explain.

The third thing left unsaid is even more puzzling. In the list of whom a man can't have sex with, with all the specifications of half sisters and sisters-in-law and granddaughters and aunts, there is no prohibition against having sex with your own daughter. It's hard to believe that is just supposed to be assumed when they very carefully spell out that you can't have sex with your own mother and explain that the reason is that she belongs to your father. Remember, back in those days the wife and children belonged to the father. They were the man's property. So, maybe property rights came first. It is another one of those things not satisfactorily explained.

So, let's just leave these mysteries hanging for right now and move on to another scripture that refers to homosexuality and see if anything gets clarified. Genesis 19:1–11 is the section of the story of Sodom and Gomorrah where the crowd comes to Lot's house demanding he give up the visitors he has, evidently so they can rape the men. But let's go back to the beginning of the story, which is at the start of chapter 18. It's really hard to date when Abraham lived, if there was a real person, and parts of this story seem similar to other, non-Israelite stories from the same or earlier times, but part of what we are hearing may be an echo of the time when people first began to live in cites and there was conflict between the older, herding, nomadic culture and the newer, and very different, social structure of people living together in large groups in these cities of maybe a thousand or more people.

Anyway, back to the story. Abraham is sitting in the shade of his tent one afternoon when he sees three men coming. He immediately gets up and runs to them, inviting them in to wash up and have a drink and a snack before they continue. The three men say sure, sounds good. So, Abraham has Sarah bake some bread, grabs a calf from the flock and has it cooked, and serves the bread and meat with some milk and curds to the three, who are sitting under a tree. The "snack" has turned into a feast.

Now, it's not clear where in this event Abraham, if ever, figures out that these are not just three ordinary men. It turns out that one of them is God and the other two seem to be avenging angels, but they evidently look and act like regular guys until they start talking to Abraham while they are eating and seem to know more than regular strangers would. First of all, they ask where Sarah is, and Abraham says she in the tent, which is evidently very close by, which is probably what was expected—close enough to pass out some more food if needed, but not actually hanging around the men. Anyway, one of the men says he will come back to visit again "at this very season," meaning in about a year, and by then Sarah will have given birth to a son. Now, Abraham and Sarah were both very old, like triple-digit old, and Sarah hadn't had a period in years, so when she hears that comment through the tent door, she laughs in her mind.

And now the guy really lets it slip that he's no ordinary Joe by asking why did Sarah laugh. So, Sarah comes out and says she didn't laugh, and he says, "Oh yes, you did." Then the men finish eating and take their leave, with Abraham walking with them a little way to see them off. And this main guy tells Abraham that he is off to deal with Sodom and Gomorrah, who evidently have committed some unspecified grave offense. So, the other two guys head on out toward Sodom, and God hangs back with Abraham.

Now, Abraham's nephew Lot and his family live in Sodom, so naturally Abraham is concerned about what might happen.

So, he begins bargaining with God, asking God if he is really going to destroy the entire city, including all the innocent people. And he bargains God down from not destroying the city if there are fifty innocent people there to not destroying the city if there are ten innocent people there. Then God leaves and Abraham goes back to his tent.

We're now at the beginning of Chapter 19, when the two "messengers," minus God, arrive in Sodom. Lot is sitting at the town gate, just like Abraham was sitting in his tent entrance, and like Abraham, he gets up to greet the visitors and invite them into his home. Remember, back then there were no deluxe motels. The travelers turn him down at first, saying they would just sleep out in the town square. But Lot insists, so they go to his house and he has a regular supper served to them, not the big feast Abraham served. But before they could go to bed for the night, the men of the city come banging on the door, demanding that the two visitors be sent out "so that we may know them," implying some kind of gang rape.

And here it starts to get pretty weird to our modern point of view. Lot goes outside, closing the door behind him, and offers to send out his two virgin daughters to be raped instead of the two men because the two men have "come under the shadow of my roof-beam." When things get weird I start checking the footnotes, and Alter comes through again, explaining that this is "the reflex of an ancient Near Eastern code in which the sacredness of the host-guest bond took precedence over all other obligations." Even today, hospitality is a major value in the culture of the Near East. The writer here is drawing parallels between the hospitality that Abraham showed as part of the nomadic herding culture, the much-reduced hospitality Lot shows while living the urban life in a city, and the ultimate inhospitality of the men of

Sodom. It would appear that, while homosexuality is not approved, the real sin of Sodom was showing a lack of hospitality to visitors.

Anyway, the men of Sodom turn down the offer of two virgins and demand the two visitors and start to threaten Lot as being a resident alien who has the temerity to judge the natives. At that point, the two visitors pull Lot back in the house, slam the door, flash a blinding light outside, sending the men of Sodom wandering around the streets no longer able to find Lot's house. The two guests tell Lot they are about to destroy the city and he should get his family and get out. Lot runs around town to the houses of his sons-in-law who married his other daughters and tried to warn them that God was about to destroy the city, but they all think it's just some strange joke. Finally, a little before dawn, he comes back alone and the two messengers tell him to take his wife and two daughters still living with him and get out of town, but he can't seem to make up his mind. The messengers grab their hands and pull them outside the city, then tell them to head for the hills and don't look back. Lot doesn't want to go up into the cliffs and caves in the rough country and asks to head to a little podunk town called Zoar, and they say, "Okay, but hurry."

So, Lot, his wife, and his two daughters make it to Zoar just after sunrise, God drops some kind of firebombs on the whole area, wiping out Sodom, Gomorrah, and everything else in the area, including all the plants. Lot's wife looks back at where they had left and turns into a pillar of salt. Meanwhile, Abraham, up above the plain with a good view, looks out and sees the smoke rising from the entire plain where the cities had been. Meanwhile, Lot decides that maybe Zoar isn't the best place to be after all and heads on up into the hills and cliffs and sets up in a cave with his two daughters.

Now, here it gets weird again. The two daughters look at their father, who has lost all his property and all his family except them, decide nobody is ever going to marry them, and decide that in order to "keep alive seed from our father," the only thing to do is get him drunk and have sex with him. Which they proceed to do—the older daughter the first night and the younger daughter the next night. We're going to skip over the question of whether a man who is so drunk he doesn't realize he's having sex with his own daughters wouldn't be too drunk to perform sexually, and finish the story. Both daughters become pregnant and have sons, one of whom becomes the founding father of Moab and the other the founding father of the Ammon. (As an aside, this story was an Israelite way of insulting Moabites and Ammonites.)

Note that there is nothing here in Genesis that says this father-daughter incest was a bad thing. It just says these two women wanted to have children and wanted to keep their family line alive, so they had sex with their father, which started two tribes of people who are still around. No comment. To understand this, remember that the big deal with Abraham and Sarah was that they didn't have children, particularly a son. The big goal in life back then was to have sons and keep the family line going. This may relate back to the belief at the time that the spirit or shade of a person went to Sheol after death and needed certain sacrifices of food and other rites to keep from fading way. It was the eldest son's duty to keep his ancestors alive in Sheol by performing the rites and offering the sacrifices.

Whether or not this is where the belief came from, there is no question that everybody, men and women, bought into the belief that having a son was the greatest thing you could do and being barren is the worst. That's why Sarah had Abraham have sex with one of her slaves and father Ishmael, just so Abraham could have a son of some kind. That's why Hannah prayed to God for a son and offered to dedicate that son to God for his whole life if she could just have a son; the result was the prophet Samuel. There was even a rule that if a married man died without a son, his closest male relative had to have sex with the widow until she had a son, who would then stand in the line of inheritance in the place his mother's first husband's son would have.

This rule comes up in Genesis 38 when Tamar's husband Er dies before they have a son, so Er's father Judah sends his second son, Onan, to "raise up seed for your brother." But Onan knew any son by Tamar would not count as his son but as his older brother's son, so he practiced an old and not very effective form of birth control known as early withdrawal and "wasted his seed on the ground." We already know that wasting seed or semen was a bad thing back then, but for the record, the sin of Onan was not masturbation but early withdrawal.

Anyway, God did not approve, Onan died, and Judah sent Tamar back home to her father, supposedly to wait for his third son to grow up but actually because he was afraid his third son would die like his first two if this third son had sex with Tamar. A long time went by, Judah didn't call Tamar back, so when she heard that Judah was going to be passing nearby she dressed up like a prostitute with a veil, sat out on the road, managed to get Judah to have sex with her and give her his seal and staff as a pledge for payment of a lamb. Tamar then goes back home with the seal and staff, not waiting around for the lamb. Three months later, it becomes obvious Tamar is pregnant, somebody tells Judah she has been sleeping around, he orders her to be burned to death, she comes up with the seal and staff proving Judah is the father, he admits that she is in the right to have sex with him since he hadn't called her back to marry his third son, the burning is called off, and Tamar has twins, one of which becomes the father of the kings of the land of Judah.

The same cultural values occupy most of the book of Ruth when Moabite Ruth's Israelite husband and both his brothers die, she goes with her mother-in-law Naomi to Israel, Naomi sends Ruth to glean grain in the field of Naomi's husband's kin Boaz, he treats her kindly, Naomi sends her back at night to "uncover his feet" and lay down. That "uncover his feet" is probably a euphemism for uncovering another body part somewhat higher up, if you get my drift. Anyway, Boaz gets the idea, but says he isn't the closest next of kin, puts Ruth off, hunts up the closest next of kin, asks him before ten witnesses if he will do his duty to Ruth and Naomi, he says no—so, long story short, Boaz does his duty, weds Ruth, and they have a son named Obed, who fathers Jesse, who fathers King David.

The point of all this discussion is that we can't always look at these laws and stories in the Old Testament with modern eyes. If you want to say that we have to take the laws in Leviticus literally as we would understand them today, then we also have to admit that we have a duty to impregnate any of our brother's wives who don't have sons when their husband dies and that father-daughter incest is okay. Frankly, I don't think most of us want to interpret our Bible that literally.

So, let's look at the other references to homosexuality in the Old Testament, keeping in mind what we have learned about the very high value the culture back then placed on having sons and being hospitable. Another passing reference is in Judges 19 and 20. In many ways, it's similar to Lot in Sodom.

Long story short: Levite from Ephraim takes a woman from Bethlehem as a concubine. She gets mad at him and goes home to Daddy in Bethlehem. Levite goes to Bethlehem to get her. Her father stalls, but eventually, the Levite leaves with the woman. It gets late, but he decides not to stop in the Jebusite town of Jebus, later known as Jerusalem, but pushes on to an Israelite town, namely Gibeah, a Benjamite Israeli town. He waits in the square, but nobody takes him in until this old Ephraimite, who lived in Gibeah, comes home from his fields and takes the Levite and the concubine in for the night.

After supper, some men of Gibeah show up and demand the guest be sent outside so they can rape him. The host says the Levite is his guest and that would be an outrage, then offers his virgin daughter instead. This deal isn't acceptable to the men, so the Levite pushes his concubine out the door and slams it behind her. They gang rape her all night, she crawls back to the door at dawn and dies. The Levite takes her body home to Ephraim, cuts it into twelve pieces, and sends one piece to each of the twelve tribes.

There is an assembly of the Israelites. The Levite says he was visiting Gibeah, the men there came to where he was a guest, intending to kill him, and ended up raping his concubine to death. The Israelites get really angry, swear never to marry their daughters to a Benjamite, raise an army, and demand that the Benjamites hand over the guys from Gibeah. The Benjamites say no way and raise their own army. Three battles are fought, the Benjamites winning the first two but getting outmaneuvered in the third. Gibeah is torched, almost all Benjamites are killed, not just the soldiers but most of the men and all the women, children, and animals. They then proceed to raze the rest of Benjamite towns, killing everybody.

Then they suddenly realize that they have basically wiped out an entire tribe of Israelites except for six hundred Benjamite men hiding in the wilderness. So, they figure out that they have to let the six hundred Benjamites come back and find them some wives so the tribe doesn't disappear. But they had all sworn not to give their daughters to Benjamites. So, they take roll and find out that nobody from Jabesh-Giliad had come to the assembly. They send the army to Jabesh-Giliad to kill everybody except the virgin women. Turns out there were only four hundred virgins in Jabesh-Giliad, but they invite the Benjamites back, give them the four hundred virgins, and tell the others to go kidnap some women from Shiloh when the women are on a pilgrimage to Bethel and take them home as wives, which gets the fathers and brothers of the women out of their oath because they are not giving the women to the Benjamites, the Benjamites are taking them. So, the Benjamites kidnap two hundred more women and everybody goes home to rebuild. End of story.

Now, obviously the points of the story are that homosexuality and genocide are bad, but killing everybody in a town to get the girls and kidnapping women are just fine if you really need a few virgins. Actually, no. The real problem with Gibeah was breaking the rules of hospitality, leaving a fellow Israelite sitting out in the town square with no place to stay, trying to kill him, then destroying his property, namely the concubine. The Levite doesn't even mention the homosexuality in his complaint to the assembly in the part that made it into the Bible, though I guess it might not have been a secret either. The point is that homosexuality was not the real problem.

Let's go on. Deuteronomy is another book of laws, probably written later than the other four books of the law. Chapter 23 starts off saying you can't marry your father's widow, even if she isn't your mother. Then it prohibits men with crushed testicles or cut-off penises from coming into the Lord's assembly.

This may have been a way of forbidding castration to make eunuchs, but it is worded to also exclude any man who had been mutilated accidently. Then chapter 23 excludes from the assembly any children of incest, any Ammonites, and any Moabites for at least ten generations. Edomites and Egyptians, on the other hand, will be okay once three generations pass.

If you are out in a camp getting ready for battle, if you have a nocturnal emission, you have to stay outside the camp the next day until sunset, when you can wash and come back in. They also have to put some kind of marker outside the camp where people have to go to defecate. You don't return runaway slaves, but give them a place to stay with you and don't mistreat them, though scholars think this was talking about foreign slaves, not other Israelite slaves, who have to be released after six years max anyway.

Then come the usually quoted verses supposedly about homosexuality. In the King James, it says, "There shall be no whore of the daughters of Israel, nor a sodomite of the sons of Israel. Thou shalt not bring the hire of a whore, or the price of a dog, into the house of the Lord thy God for any vow; for even both these are abomination unto the Lord thy God." The New English translation renders this as "No Israelite woman shall become a temple prostitute, and no Israelite man shall prostitute himself in this way. You shall not allow a common prostitute's fee, or the fee of a male prostitute, to be brought into the house of the Lord your God in fulfilment of any vow, for both of them are abominable to the Lord your God." Robert Alter, the guy with the footnotes, tenders this as, "There shall be no cult-harlot from the daughters of Israel, and there shall be no cult-catamite from the sons of Israel. You shall not bring a whore's pay nor a dog's price to the house of the Lord your God for any votive offering, for both of them are the abhorrence for the Lord your God."

Then the chapter goes on to forbid charging your brother interest on any loans, but saying it's okay to charge foreigners interest, that you should keep your vows, and that if you go into somebody else's vineyard, you can eat your fill of the grapes but not take any home, and pluck grain from somebody else's field by hand but you can't reap it with a sickle.

But back to the sex. The terms variously translated as "whore" and "sodomite" or "temple prostitute," or "cult-harlot" and "cult-catamite" are *qedeshah* and *qadesh* in the old Hebrew. Their meaning is, to quote Alter, "disputed." At various places and times back then, there were temples, usually associated with fertility goddesses, where women, and sometimes men, were associated with the temple as prostitutes, providing sexual services as part of the religion. Since it was the men who made the sacrifices at these temples, the male prostitutes would have been providing homosexual services. Whether that kind of thing was going on in Israel with some of the other gods who hadn't been kicked out yet is not clear.

At any rate, the root of both *qedeshah* and *qadesh* means "sacred," so these people are not just your ordinary, run-of-the-mill prostitutes, no matter the gender. The important thing here seems to be the association with a fertility cult, meaning a god or goddess besides Yahweh. It's not the homosexuality that's the problem; it's the association with worship of another deity. It's the same thing with the references in First Kings 14:24, 15:12, 22:46, and Second Kings 23:7. The problem is not male prostitution; it's prostitution associated with worship of another god.

That's pretty much it for the Old Testament. Basically, I would call it a draw. Nobody has anything good to say about homosexuality, but what is said is so much in the context of a culture that approved father-daughter incest, passing women from brother to brother until they had a son, mass murder, and kidnapping women that I really don't think we want to live in a world with those values anymore. We would like to think that both we and Christianity have moved out from under the law of the Old Testament and into the grace of the New Testament. So, let's see what the New Testament says about homosexuality.

However, as we have noted, Jesus doesn't say anything at all about it. There's not much question that the Jewish culture of the New Testament era was not fond of homosexuality, at least in males, probably due to the problem with wasting seed or taking on a female role. But Greek culture was just fine with homosexuality among males, and Roman culture didn't have any real problems with it. The Romans were more worried about people of different classes having sex than they were about the gender of the people having sex. Paul, as the apostle to the Gentiles, would be the one expected to have to deal with that conflict and, indeed, in his letters is the only place we find any reference to homosexuality. But there are still only two references.

Let's start with the one in First Corinthians. In chapter 6, Paul is railing against the Christians in Corinth who are taking fellow Christians to court to settle business disputes. Paul says conflicts between Christians should be settled within the community, not by pagan law. He says it would be better to just let yourself be robbed than go to court, then accuses the Corinthian Christians of injuring and robbing their fellow Christians. He then says, "Surely you know that the unjust will never come into the possession of the kingdom of God. Make no mistake: no fornicator or idolater, none who are guilty either of adultery or of homosexual perversion, no thieves or grabber or drunkards or slanderers or swindlers will possess the kingdom of God. Such were some of you. But you have been through the purifying waters;

you have been dedicated to God and justified through the name of the Lord Jesus and the Spirit of God." Paul then anticipates the Corinthians' objection that, since they have been saved, they are free of sin and are free to do anything. Paul agrees but says that while you are free to do anything, not everything is good for us.

He then launches into his famous lines about our bodies being raised as Jesus was raised, so they belong to Christ and are the dwelling place of the Holy Spirit, so fornication is a particularly bad sin because it is a sin against one's own body. He concludes this section with, "You do not belong to yourselves; you were bought at a price. Then honor God in your body." But what might provide some insight into this is the next section, in Chapter 7:

> "It is a good thing for a man to have nothing to do with women; but because there is so much immorality, let each man have his own wife and each woman her own husband. The husband must give the wife what is due to her, and the wife equally must give the husband his due. The wife cannot claim her body as her own; it is her husband's. Equally, the husband cannot claim his body as his own; it is his wife's. Do not deny yourselves to one another, except when you agree upon a temporary abstinence in order to devote yourselves to prayer; afterwards you may come together again; otherwise, for lack of self-control, you may be tempted by Satan. All this I say by way of concession, not command. I should like you all to be as I am myself; but everyone has the gift God has granted him, one this gift and another that. To the unmarried and to widows I say this: it is a good thing if they stay as I am myself; but if they

cannot control themselves, they should marry. Better to be married than burn with vain desire. To the married I give this ruling, which is not mine but the Lord's; a wife must not separate herself from her husband; if she does, she must either remain unmarried or be reconciled to her husband; and the husband must not divorce his wife."

Paul then goes on to discuss what to do if one spouse is a Christian and the other is not and what to do about circumcision and slavery related to becoming a Christian. He admits he has no instructions from the Lord about celibacy, but is generally in favor of it. The key phrase comes in verse 29: "What I mean, my friends, is this. The time we live in will not last long"; and in verse 31: "For the whole frame of this world is passing away."

So, let's review: First, this section is not about homosexuality. Homosexuality is only mentioned as one of several things that will keep you out of heaven, along with fornication, robbery, drunkenness, slander, and, depending on which translation you look at, maybe usury and having a foul mouth. The main point Paul is trying to make is that Christians have to settle their own problems, not haul them off to some pagan institution. The second thing is that Paul really seems to be anti-sex. He's not only against prostitution and fornication; he's not even that fond of sex within marriage, accepting it only to avoid something worse. And to my mind, the real key to understanding Paul is to recognize, as he states plainly, that he is expecting the Second Coming just any day now. He admits that some of this is just his advice, not orders from God, but his advice is predicated on Jesus coming back very, very soon. His whole idea is to just leave things as they are for right now because we won't have to put up with the way things are very long and we need to keep as pure and holy as we can until the Lord arrives.

Now, there are times when I am tempted to think that Jesus did come back sometime early in the second century and we are all living in hell now, but usually, I go with the idea that if there is a Second Coming, it hasn't happened yet. Which means I am stuck trying to figure out when Paul thought he was speaking with the authority of God and when he was just spouting his own advice and how much either of those depended on the idea that there wasn't going to be a tomorrow. While there are advantages to living as if Jesus could come back tonight, after two thousand years, I have to think the odds are against it and long-term planning is not a bad idea. So, we have a vote for putting homosexuality in the no category along with sex outside of marriage and getting drunk and a great big warning that we cannot assume the New Testament was not influenced by the times and cultures in which it was written any less than the Old Testament.

This is something we need to keep in mind as we go to the last scriptural reference to homosexuality: Romans chapter 1. After all the greetings and thanks, and apologies for not dropping in to visit yet, Paul starts talking about divine retribution:

> "For we see divine retribution revealed from heaven and falling upon all the godless wickedness of men. In their wickedness they are stifling the truth. For all that may be known of God by men lies plain before their eyes; indeed God himself has disclosed it to them. His invisible attributes, that is to say his everlasting power and deity, have been visible, ever since the world began, to the eye of reason, in the things he has made. There is therefore no possible defense of

their conduct; knowing God, they refused to honour him as God, or to render him thanks. Hence all their thinking has ended in futility, and their misguided minds are plunged in darkness. They boast of their wisdom, but they have made fools of themselves, exchanging the splendor of immortal God for an image shaped like mortal man, even for images like birds, beasts, and creeping things. For this reason God has given them up to the vileness of their own desires, and the consequent degradation of their bodies, because they have bartered away the true God for a false one, and have offered reverence and worship to created things instead of to the Creator, who is blessed forever; amen. In consequence, I say, god has given them up to shameful passions. Their women have exchanged natural intercourse for unnatural, and their men, in turn, giving up natural relations with women, burn with lust for one another; males behave indecently with males, and are paid in their own persons the fitting wage of such perversion. Thus, because they have not seen fit to acknowledge God, he has given them up to their own depraved reason. This leads them to break all rules of conduct. They are filled with every kind of injustice, mischief, rapacity, and malice. They are one mass of envy, murder, rivalry, treachery, and malevolence; whisperers and scandal-mongers, hateful to God, insolent, arrogant, and boastful; they invent new kinds of mischief, they show no loyalty to parents, no conscience, no fidelity to their plighted word; they are without natural affection and without pity. They know well enough the just decree of God, that those who behave like this deserve to die, and yet they do it; not only so, they actually applaud such practices. You therefore have no defense—you who sit in judgement, whoever you may be—for in judging your fellow-man you condemn yourself, since you, the judge, are equally guilty. It is admitted that God's judgement is rightly passed upon all who commit such crimes as these; and do you imagine—you who pass judgement on the guilty while committing the same crimes yourself—do you imagine that you, any more than they, will escape the judgement of God?"

Now, this is, as usual with Paul, a complex passage, but the big thing to notice here is that homosexuality is not the sin, it is the punishment. The sin is idolatry. Paul is saying that God's power and deity are obvious from his creation, yet people have refused to worship God the Creator and have instead worshipped created things, images shaped like humans or even animals, probably referring to the statues of the gods in the various Roman temples. The Romans weren't actually worshipping the statues any more than Christians worship a wooden cross; rather they worshipped the deity the statue represented, but none of these Roman gods were creator gods.

Anyway, because of this refusal to worship the Creator, God has given the people up to their own desires and they are paid the fitting wage for their shameful passions. The J. B. Phillips paraphrase of the New Testament has this as they receive "in their personalities the consequence of sexual perversity." In parallel with this, Paul says that because they have not acknowledged God, not admitted God to their consciousness, he has turned them over to their depraved reason, to their corrupt minds, which leads them to all kinds of rule-breaking and iniquity, from murder to defying your parents. And it is this second list of bad things that leads to death.

Now, obviously, this is not a vote in favor of homosexuality. It even seems to be the only time anything in the Bible is against female homosexuality, though it's not terribly specific. But the implication is that homosexuality is the result of a deeper alienation from God and carries its own penalty, perhaps unlike the second list of iniquities.

Now at this point, a lot of people would say this is a cultural artifact, something coming out of the ancient science of the time. Today, we know that homosexuality is not really a choice but is possibly determined by the size of certain brain structures as determined by the timing and amount of hormones released during fetus development in the womb or some other biological cause. And we can get into whether these hormone fluctuations are random or caused by stress or other environmental effects on the mother during pregnancy or whether there is a genetic element that decreases evolutionary reproductive fitness in males but increases it in their female relatives and thus persists. And others would reply that the very cultures Paul was writing to, with their more widespread practice of homosexuality than today, would argue against the claim that homosexuality is biologically determined but must have some cultural and individual component. To which the first group would reply that the second group has a too simplistic view of sexuality, that sexuality is not an either-or but a range, even for heterosexuals, within which a certain flexibility is natural—that female sexuality tends to be a little more flexible than male, but even males have a malleability within the biological range ordained by their genes and in-utero development. And all of them would probably be right about some things and wrong about others. But I don't want to get into that.

Let us just agree that there is some biological component to homosexuality that Paul and the other people back in the first century did not fully appreciate, so we have to take these kinds of pronouncements by Paul with a grain of salt, realizing that he was trying to express something about a god beyond understanding while using the very restricted language and concepts and cultures of the time, which are not our languages, concepts, or cultures. Let's just agree that Paul thought worshipping a god or gods who were not the Creator God was not a good idea and caused lots of problems and move on to what he said next.

What he said next was that we are in no position to judge; that's God's job. We are just as guilty before God as those other guys and have no business judging them. Paul says we will all get our judgment day before God, so we better be very careful who we condemn, because we will all be judged by the same God.

So, what do we say about homosexuality after all this? We can say it is not a subject of major concern in the Bible, with only six significant references. We can say those references all seem to be heavily influenced by the culture and lack of scientific understanding of biology of the time. We can say that most of the references are to male homosexuality and that female homosexuality is barely mentioned at all, probably because of the analogous thinking of the culture that assumed the male semen—like seeds—somehow contained the basics of life, and that life was being wasted or even killed if it was not ejaculated into a female's vagina.

In short, while the Bible is clearly not in favor of homosexuality, all the condemnations of it are so closely tied to the cultural or temporal elements of the references that they provide poor guidance to us today.

Today, we have to decide what we believe about the morality of homosexuality based on what we know today, not on some literal reading of a few verses taken out of the context of the time they were written. We have to decide about homosexuality based on what we now know about its biological influences and the complexity of sexuality in general, which is far more complex than just XX or XY genes. We have to decide based on Paul's command not to judge others. We have to decide based on Jesus's command to love one another. That is how we have to decide.

Amen.

Sermon Five

Evil

I would like to propose to you a new definition of "evil." Now, I looked in my *Webster's Unabridged* and it had almost a third of a column on various meanings of the word "evil," which was interesting but I didn't think you wanted to hear me read all that. So, I dug out my old *Thorndike Barnhart* high school dictionary, which says evil is "morally bad, wrong, sinful, wicked, causing harm or injury, unfortunate, due to bad character or conduct." So, I guess the first thing I need to do is clarify what kind of evil I am talking about. I'm not talking about the evil hurricane or earthquake that causes lots of harm or injury. That kind of natural disaster creates too many theological problems for anybody to deal with.

For example, back in 1755 in Lisbon, Portugal, a massive earthquake struck on All Saints' Day while most people were in church. Fissures up to fifteen feet wide opened up, some under churches. Churches collapsed onto their congregations all over town. People who survived rushed to open spaces like the docks and shoreline, only to watch the sea recede and then rush back in a series of tsunamis, killing most of the people on the shore. This was followed by a series of fires that destroyed hundreds more buildings and killed even more people.

Estimates of the dead in Lisbon alone range up to one hundred thousand people, with thousands more dead across Portugal and into Spain and Morocco. That one hundred thousand for Lisbon alone is probably on the high side, but even if it was only fifty thousand, that's still one out of four people since there were probably only about two hundred thousand people living in the city at the time. All of Europe and parts of North Africa felt the quake, and the tsunami reached as far as Brazil. It was one of the deadliest earthquakes of all time and prompted some real soul-searching throughout Europe. It was noted that almost all the churches in Lisbon were destroyed, but the red-light district suffered comparatively little damage. If this was a judgment of God, it seemed a little strange—and challenged a lot of people's faith in God.

Voltaire decided that maybe not all things work out for the best under God's care and wrote *Candide* as a counterexample to this best of all possible worlds, including the earthquake as part of the book. Rousseau decided the earthquake was caused by too many people living in cities and promoted a more natural way of living and his "noble savage." Kant published a theory of what caused earthquakes, which was wrong but was the beginning of the science of seismology. Basically, the question everybody was wrestling with was how could a good God cause or even allow such an evil event to occur.

Today, we have a much better idea of what causes earthquakes, with the theory of tectonic plates floating slowly around and bumping into each other in one place and separating in another. We have also come to realize that nature and the universe generally do their own thing without God pushing every little button. Otherwise, we would have to blame God for every flood, hurricane, earthquake, tsunami, lightning strike, forest fire, and every other natural disaster. We could also make a pretty good case that God was responsible for at least some automobile accidents, cases of cancer, birth defects, and childhood diseases. All you have to do is walk down the hall in any of our children's hospitals to find plenty of evidence of this kind of harm and injury.

If this kind of thing is evil, and if God is really the sole creator and in total control and ultimately responsible for the system itself, then God created the system and God created evil. Even if you believe Satan is behind all this, if God created everything, then God created Satan and the buck still stops at God. Otherwise, Satan had some kind of independent creation and God is not in total control. So, do we really want to lay every unfortunate incident on God's head?

In fact, it always bothers me when somebody crawls out of the rubble of a tornado or something and blesses God for saving them when there were other people in the building who died. Do they really believe God chose to save them but kill the others? If so, why? Were they better people? Not much evidence of that, in general. Do they have some unfulfilled purpose that the other people didn't? If that's true, I think a lot of us would question God's choices, especially when the dead include babies and little children. I think we would really be making a mistake to give God credit or blame for these things that are basically natural events or the results of chance. But I think this mindless, purposeless kind of event, while terrible and causing untold death and suffering, is not really what we or the Bible mean by evil.

At least, this is not the kind of evil I want to talk about. These kinds of naturally occurring events, we can blame God for or not, but generally, we just get ourselves in all kinds of theological and philosophical trouble if we do.

No, what I want to talk about is the evil that men do–or, to keep my language up-to-date, the evil that human beings do. Evil that somewhere along the line has one or more human beings behind it, making some kind of choice. The evil that is caused by people who are "morally bad, wrong, sinful, wicked, due to bad character or conduct." What I am proposing is that this evil, at its base, is caused by one person or a group of people deciding that another person or group of people are so different from them that the same rules don't apply to the second group.

An obvious example is the Nazis, who decided that Jews, Roma (known in WWII as Gypsies), homosexuals, and even some Poles were so different from them that it was just fine to do things to them that the Nazis would never have dreamed of doing to other people like themselves. We can say something similar about the chattel slavery of the South before the Civil War, where preachers even preached from the pulpit that Blacks were so different and deficient, as descendants of Ham, that they needed to be controlled by whites. Sad to say, there are even some people today who believe that Blacks are so different from whites that the rules should be different for them. Today, we also hear many people saying similar things about various types of immigrants, as if they aren't quite human enough to feel the same pain when their families are torn apart as we would feel.

But we can also bring this down to a much more local level. Some places have problems with gangs, which, by definition, are one group of people saying that those in the gang are somehow different from those outside the gang and have to play the game of life by different rules. What are bullies except people who think other people are weaker somehow, or less worthy, and hence fair game to be treated differently? Or we can go back to the snake in the Garden of Eden telling Eve that Yahweh is treating her differently by not letting her eat of the Tree of Knowledge so she can't become like the other gods. Isn't most crime somebody saying the rules don't apply to me, either because those in power won't let me play by the same rules they do or because the rules are hurting me more than I can take?

Now, I am not so simple as to not think that a lot of conflicts are caused by people disagreeing about what the rules are. Culture clashes are very real and lead to a lot of wars. The rules on the street are not the same as the rules in a court of law. But doesn't the evil grow out of the decision that one person or group isn't enough like us to follow the same set of rules?

If you look at languages, the name people give to their tribe usually means the people or the humans or the real ones. Their names for other groups tend to be insults, implying they are not real people or are subhuman in some way. Hence, it is just fine to kill them. After all, they are not really human people, like us. Even after we stopped living in tribes, we kept trying to define who is us and who is other, because the rules were different for "others." So, we have nations and ethnicities and races and denominations and religions—and however we define ourselves, it's us against them.

One of the very valid complaints about radical Islam is that they sometimes claim it is okay to treat non-Muslims differently from Muslims. Of course, Christians are in no position to talk, having done the same kind of thing from the Crusades down to the present day when some of us claim to live in a Christian nation, as if nobody else has a right to live here. We also have a bad habit of dividing the groups even finer, with terrible results. On St. Bartholomew's Day in 1572, French Catholics killed between five thousand and ten thousand French Protestants in one day, which is probably more Christians than the Romans killed in all the persecutions during the entire Roman Empire. Of course, Protestants have returned the favor, even rioting and burning down Irish Catholic churches in Philadelphia as late as the 1800s when so many Irish came over to escape the Potato Famine. We look for people who we can claim are different in some way and then make them targets for attack or subjugation.

Now, I could come up with thousands more examples, probably picking some out of today's newspaper, especially looking for stories about immigrants or police shootings. Other examples are as close as the nearest history book. But I hope I have made my point, that considering others as somehow different enough to have a different set of rules applied just leads to very bad things. One of the recurring themes in science fiction is that it will be a good thing to find alien life because it will make all of us here on this planet realize we really are one group and the aliens will become the "other." I'm not sure it will be that easy, but that's enough to get my vote in support of funding searches for extraterrestrial life in hopes of solving some of our conflicts down here.

Beyond that, I am not claiming I know any solution to evil. I don't know how we can stop thinking of "us" and "them." Perhaps some of the atheist philosophers have a point that the separation of people into "us and them" is inherent in human nature.

I guess what I would like to say is that if we want to oppose or prevent evil, one of the things we have to do is recognize when we ourselves are classifying people as "other" in some way. One of the more useful ideals we as Americans hold is that all people are equal before the law. Now, anybody who knows anything about the history of law or crime and punishment in America knows that this is an ideal, not a fact. It has not been and is not now the way the justice system actually works. Look up "The Justice Project" on the internet and read about all the innocent people sent to prison or death because they did not get equal justice before the law.

But it is a great ideal that we should strive for and believe in. What I am suggesting is that we expand this ideal beyond the legal system. We already claim that all are equal before the throne of God. Supposedly within Christianity, there is no Jew or Greek, male or female. Can we at least become a little more aware of when we are drawing a line between us and some other person or group?

I'm not saying there won't be disagreements about what the rules of life should be—of course, there will be. There are also inevitable conflicts about who gets to make the rules and how that gets done. And as long as human beings are making the rules, some of those rules are going to be just plain bad rules, inherently unjust and unfair, based on misunderstandings of culture or psychology, and counterproductive in the long run. Making the rules is a never-ending process, and there is always need for improvement. But what I am saying is that we should agree that the rules of life should be the same for everybody.

Let's get away from this idea that somebody who is different somehow has to play by a different set of rules. Whether it's as obvious as racial prejudice or as subtle as these religious freedom movements in state legislatures, it is saying that one person or group is different and doesn't get to play by the same rules as I do. Sooner or later, somewhere down the line, the result is evil, and we need to recognize it and prevent as much of it as we can, for our own sake.

Amen.

Sermon Six

The Last Supper

There is a mystery about the Last Supper. Actually, there are a puzzle, a theological issue, and a mystery. The puzzle is when it happened. The Gospels of Mark, Matthew, and Luke say the crucifixion happened on the Friday of Passover, but the Gospel of John says it was on the "day of preparation" for Passover, which would have been a Thursday. So, the Last Supper would have been the evening before, either the Wednesday or Thursday, which makes a difference because on Thursday it would have been the actual Passover meal, while on Wednesday it would have been more like an ordinary supper. Some people say John changed the day because he saw Jesus as the symbolic "Passover Lamb" killed for the sins of the world, so Jesus had to actually die on the day of Passover. Others say Mark, Matthew, and Luke just got it wrong because a lot of the other things John says about the last days seem more aware of the details.

Actually, this is just one example of a long list of discrepancies between John and the other Gospels. For example, Mark, Matthew, and Luke have Jesus driving the money changers out of the temple during the week before his crucifixion, but John puts that event way earlier, at the beginning of Jesus's ministry. John also disagrees with Matthew and Mark about which night it was that Mary, of Martha and Mary and Lazarus, anointed Jesus's feet with nard. Also, John says Jesus was crucified around noon, the other three writers say it was about nine o'clock in the morning. There are also huge sections of John that are not in the other three Gospels and, vice versa, sections of the other three that are not in John. The Gospel of John seems to have come from what is called an "independent tradition."

Let's take time for a little history lesson here. Okay, a *long* history lesson. If you look at Roman and Jewish sources outside the Bible for when Pilate was in charge in Jerusalem, Herod was in charge of Galilee, Caiaphas was High Priest, and other historical references like that, Jesus was probably crucified somewhere around year 33, plus or minus a year or two, maybe three. The earliest writing we have about Jesus actually comes from Paul's letters, which were probably written in the 50s and early 60s, but even there you have to be careful because not all the letters in the New Testament that have Paul's name on them were actually written by Paul. Some of those letters were written later by other people who claimed they were written by Paul to make them sound more authoritative.

We can tell this in a variety of ways—for example, writing style. It's like reading a bunch of novels by William Faulkner, then somebody handing you a novel with Faulkner's name on it but actually written by Earnest Hemmingway. They just don't sound the same. This kind of difference in writing style can be analyzed by computer programs that look at vocabulary used, length of sentences, use of clauses, and other characteristics to determine if some given text was written by the same person who wrote some other text. The real Paul had a tendency, even in Greek, to write long, complex sentences with lots of clauses and interjected phrases and somewhat unclear internal referents. If something is simple and clear, it probably wasn't written by Paul.

We can also look at things like allusions to events or people that Paul would never have known about and theological questions that didn't come up while he was alive that are discussed by the pseudo-Pauls in their letters, as well as when references to the various letters start showing up in other writings. Most biblical scholars say Romans, 1 and 2 Corinthians, Galatians, Philippians, 1 Thessalonians, and Philemon were probably written by the real Paul. There is a lot of disagreement about Ephesians and Colossians but most people who study this kind of thing think Hebrews, 2 Thessalonians, 1 and 2 Timothy, and Titus were probably written by pseudo-Pauls years after the real Paul died. (As an aside, if we accept this separation, some church historians speculate that Hebrews was written by the Priscilla that Paul refers to in his real letters but her authorship was deliberately suppressed and the text attributed to Paul. At any rate, the real Paul seemed to be pretty flexible concerning the activities of women in the very early and informal church, while the other pseudo-Pauls were more interested in reestablishing definite gender roles in the later, more established and hierarchical church.)

Fortunately for us—back to talking about the Last Supper—the earliest description of the Last Supper is in one of the letters written by the real Paul, namely 1 Corinthians 11:23–25. We've all heard it before.

> "For I have received of the Lord that which also I delivered unto you. That the Lord Jesus the same night in which he was betrayed took bread: and when he had given thanks, he brake it, and said, Take, eat: this is my body, which is broken for you: this do in remembrance of me. After the same manner also he took the cup, when he had supped, saying, This cup is the new testament in my blood: this do ye, as oft as ye drink it, in remembrance of me.

> For as often as ye eat this bread, and drink this cup,
> ye do shew the Lord's death till he come."

Unfortunately, it's only these three verses in the middle of a diatribe against the way the Christians in Corinth were not sharing food, some feasting and others going hungry, when celebrating the Last Supper and some were getting drunk. It evidently wasn't a little bite of bread and sip of juice back then.

Which brings us to a really long history lesson. For the real details of the Last Supper, we have to wait for the Gospels to be written. The first of these was Mark, probably written sometime around year 70, either a few years before or after the destruction of Jerusalem by the Romans, based on some references in Mark to war in Judea and persecution.

Now, just to be clear, we don't really know who wrote any of the Gospels. There is no author's name in the text of any of them and they weren't ascribed to anybody until years later, usually in the next century. Papias of Hierapolis (c. AD 125) ascribes this early Gospel to Mark the Evangelist, possibly the same as the John Mark who may have been a cousin of Barnabas and went with Paul on his first missionary journey, but skipped out on him partway through for unclear reasons. Later, he supposedly became an interpreter for Peter when Peter left Jerusalem for Greek-speaking parts and gets his information about Jesus from Peter. Most scholars today think Papias didn't know what he was talking about and was just trying to give the Gospel a credible-sounding source. Based on the text, it was probably written by a Jew, but for a Greek audience, since he has to explain certain Jewish references and Aramaic translations.

Just to be clear, this is probably not the first writing about Jesus. Based on comparisons of Mark, Matthew, and Luke, plus references in later, non-biblical sources, there were already collections of sayings of Jesus on various topics, as well as purely oral history. Mark, or whoever, evidently used some of these sayings' sources, oral histories, and whatever whoever might have gotten from Peter to compile this Gospel of Mark.

Mark is sort of the bare-bones Gospel. There are no nativity stories and the oldest manuscripts we have actually end at chapter 16, verse 8, with the women running off from the empty tomb. The verses after that were evidently added later by somebody who didn't like the ending. No post-resurrection stories in Mark.

The Gospel of Matthew was probably written next, sometime between years 80 and 90, give or take. Papias again is the first person we know of to claim it was written by Matthew, by which he would have meant Matthew the Apostle, one of the Twelve, the erstwhile tax collector. As a "publican," Matthew would at least probably have been literate, but if the dating is right, he would have been in his eighties or nineties when this Gospel was written, so again, it sounds good to have an apostle writing a Gospel, but it isn't likely.

It was written in Greek, but whoever wrote it was almost certainly Jewish and writing to a group of Jewish Christians, probably in Asia Minor. Remember that at first the followers of Jesus still considered themselves Jews and followed the Jewish laws while still considering Jesus the Messiah.

The leader of the church in Jerusalem was James—the brother of Jesus, not the Apostle—and this James was a Nazarite, a sort of radical Jew who didn't cut his beard or have sex. James was a major figure in the political events leading up to the Jewish revolt, at least until he was tossed off the top of the temple in year 62. Josephus, in his history of the revolt, actually says more about James than about Jesus, who only gets a line or two and some of that may have been added later. Some of these Jewish Christians may have stayed in Jerusalem to fight the Romans, and there are whispers of rumors that there may have been a few at Masada, the Jewish last stand, but a lot of them headed for the hills before the Romans surrounded the city, according to the ancient historians of Christianity, following a prophecy given to some of the church elders, and hiding out as a group in Pella, a town on the other side of the Jordan River a ways north of Jerusalem and out of the path of the Roman army.

Anyway, these were not the only Jewish Christians. After the revolt was put down, there were other groups scattered around in the Jewish Diaspora that followed the destruction of Jerusalem that Matthew, whoever he was, seemed to be writing to.

Whoever Matthew was, he had a copy of the Gospel of Mark to copy, using 600 of the 661 verses in Mark, with minor edits, plus adding material from a sayings collection called "Q" that Mark did not use, and some of his own stuff from wherever he got it. But Matthew is not just compiling sources and editing them together. He is interested in communicating Jesus's teachings more than just his acts. He wants to show Jesus as the Messiah, to set his church off from the other Jews, and so emphasizes Jesus's messianic qualities. Thus, we get nativity stories and other materials intended to present Jesus as the fulfillment of Old Testament prophecies.

Next came the Gospel of Luke, sometime between year 80 and 110, which is actually the first part of a two-part text, the second part being the Acts of the Apostles. Now, there was a guy named Luke who was a Greek physician who went with Paul on some of his later journeys, and that is who early historians of Christianity later claimed wrote the Gospel of Luke and

Acts. The problem is that some of the things Luke says in Acts about Paul don't jive with what Paul says in his real letters.

For example, Paul, in Galatians 1, claims that he stayed unknown to Christians in Judea after his conversion, but Acts tells a very different story. Luke's theology is also very different from what is in Paul's letters on some points, and in Acts, he sometimes presents Paul as having theological opinions that disagree with what Paul says in his letters. There are just so many discrepancies that it's hard to believe whoever wrote the Gospel of Luke actually was with Paul for years. So again, we don't know who wrote the Gospel of Luke or Acts.

Whoever it was, he seems to have been a Greek, writing in Greek, for an audience of Greeks. Like Matthew, he had a copy of Mark and of "Q" as the basis for his Gospel, plus some of his own unique information and viewpoint to add. He modeled his structure on other Greek and Roman writers of histories, including Josephus, tried to include complete speeches of Jesus and the Apostles (even if he had to edit them together from sayings), went from birth to death and resurrection, and seemed to have a focus on the conflicts between rich and poor and, naturally, on whether "foreigners" could be included in Christianity.

Then, sort of out of left field, comes the Gospel of John. Even though it seems to have been written a little later than the other Gospels, between year 90 and 110 at least, it isn't based on Mark or "Q" or even on Matthew or Luke. If you get what's called a "Parallel New Testament," where they try to line up the corresponding verses from the four Gospels side by side, you will see that there are huge chunks of John that aren't in any of the other three Gospels, and just as big chunks of the other three that are not in John. John seems to be getting his information from other sources, but exactly where is not clear. There is a lot of overlap in events told about, but even there, as we noticed about the Last Supper and the Crucifixion, the details are different.

Some of the sayings of Jesus found only in John seem to be older than the other Gospels, and John seems to know more about the actual geography of Jerusalem than the others, some of his details about the lead-up to the crucifixion (such as the prior meeting of the Jewish authorities) are more historically plausible, and his putting the Last Supper and the crucifixion a day earlier than the other Gospels may even be more accurate.

So, who was this John? The legend is that the "Beloved Disciple" referred to in chapter 21 as the author was John the Apostle, hence we are getting a first-person account. But John the Apostle was an Aramaic-speaking fisherman who, at best, would have been semiliterate. It's possible he could have learned to write classical Greek like a philosopher later in life, and he certainly would have had time because he would have to have been nearly ninety years old or older by the time he got around to writing this Gospel.

Scholars today think there may actually have been two or three authors, possibly writing years apart, creating layers upon layers of text through various editions of the Gospel. And while whoever wrote John seems to have been a Jew and very knowledgeable about Jewish law, the emphasis is very definitely on how Christianity and Judaism have now split apart into opposing religions as Christianity becomes more and more a religion of Gentiles. And the current consensus is that whoever wrote the Gospel of John is not the same as the John who wrote Revelations.

One wild guess about the John who wrote the Gospel comes from Hugh Schonfield, a translator of the New Testament, who suggests that it is possible that a guy known as John the Elder (as in "Elder of the church")—who church historian Eusebius says has a tomb in Ephesus and was still alive in year 140—could have written the Gospel of John and the Letters of John, after getting his information from John the Priest, who was a Jewish priest turned Christian, who was the real "Beloved Disciple," not John the Apostle, and who lived in Ephesus, wrote Revelations and lived to a great age. Eusebius quotes Polycrates, bishop of Ephesus, as writing that "John, who rested on the bosom of our Lord, who was a priest that wore the sacerdotal plate, witness and teacher, he, also (like John the Elder) rests at Ephesus," meaning both Johns are buried there.

Wherever whoever wrote the Gospel of John got his information, it is evident that a good part of it was not from the same places Mark, Matthew, and Luke got theirs—they were all writing forty to eighty years after the fact, were almost certainly not eyewitnesses, and had their own axes to grind. So, the puzzle of whether the Last Supper was on Wednesday or Thursday just reveals that there are a lot of discrepancies between the Gospels, the Acts, and even the Letters of Paul, so we better not get too hung up on the details or try to pretend there is some way to make all these various sources agree on everything.

Which brings us to the theological issue. This is the idea of transubstantiation. "Trans" means across, as in "transatlantic" or "transportation." "Substantiation" is from the same root as "substance." So, we have "across substances," to go from one substance to another. Therefore, transubstantiation is the theological idea that the bread and the wine offered in the sacrifice of the sacrament of the Eucharist change substance and become, in reality, the Body and Blood of Jesus the Christ. At times, this idea has gotten Christians accused of cannibalism. And if you were to take this idea literally, that accusation would probably be right.

Fortunately, a literal interpretation of this scripture is demonstrably false. No matter where in the process of praying over, distributing, or even eating the bread and wine that you stop to examine them, from just looking at them to putting them into a mass spectrometer, does the bread change to human meat or the wine into human blood. Now, the people way back when knew this. The word "transubstantiation" isn't even used until Hildebert de Lavardin, Archbishop of Tours, used it in the eleventh century. By the end of the twelfth century, however, the term was in widespread use. The Fourth Council of the Lateran, which convened beginning November 11, 1215, spoke of the bread and wine as "transubstantiated" into the Body and Blood of Christ: "His body and blood are truly contained in the sacrament of the altar under the forms of bread and wine, the bread and wine having been *transubstantiated*, by God's power, into his body and blood."

Note those words "under the forms of bread and wine." The idea was that the part of the bread and wine that you could see or touch or taste or smell stayed the same, but, in some mysterious way, "the signs of bread and wine become, in a way surpassing understanding, the Body and Blood of Christ." They got into all kinds of philosophical discussions about the differences between the forms and the signs, or the species and the substance, or the appearance and the essence. The idea, again, being that even though the outward appearance had not changed, something about the spiritual essence had.

Then along came the Protestants, who claimed at one extreme that the whole thing was just a symbol, a ritual used to remember the sacrifice of Jesus, and that nothing actually changed, with various Protestant theologians, sects, and eventually denominations staking out various positions between the two extremes of changed spiritual substance to just another symbol. Of course, it was this kind of splitting theological hairs that led to wars and massacres of Christians by Christians. Exactly what the difference is between saying something doesn't physically change but only spiritually changes and saying something changes symbolically is beyond my poor brain, but people still seem to be willing to kill each other over it, or at least not share Communion with whoever says the opposite. So, that's the big theological issue related to the Last Supper.

Which brings us to the real mystery. If you accept the idea that what Jesus was doing was saying his death on the cross was going to be a sacrifice, during which he accepted the punishment for our sins, that his body was broken and his blood was shed for us, like the animals sacrificed in the temple in atonement for sins, then you have a real problem. The problem is not in the idea of a sacrifice being killed to pay for our sins or the idea of somebody taking on the sins of people like a scapegoat—that's all good Old Testament stuff. It's not even when Jesus says to eat his body. It's when Jesus says to drink his blood. That's like telling every Jew in the room to break one of their strongest taboos. We're so used to hearing it that we don't recognize the power of what Jesus is saying. And why Jesus would use that absolutely blasphemous image is a great mystery.

Let's go back and look at the laws about sacrifices in the temple. If you brought an animal to the temple, the priest would take it, kill it according to the procedure specified in the laws laid out in Leviticus, and divide the body into pieces. Certain parts of the body got tossed into the fire, the holocaust. For some sacrifices, other cuts of the meat would go to the temple and show up on the menu in the dining hall that night; that was part of the way the priests got paid. For some types of sacrifices, the person making the sacrifice would even get some of the meat back so they could have a little feast of their own at supper that night. So, the idea of eating part of the sacrifice, properly cooked and maybe with a little salt and pepper, was not that unusual an idea. But drinking the blood was.

The first time God told people not to eat or drink blood was actually back in Genesis, in chapter 9, verse 4, where God lays out some rules for Noah and his family after the flood. "But flesh with its lifeblood still in it you shall not eat." It's this idea that blood was life that influenced the dietary laws that came later. Leviticus says the blood of sacrifices is to be drained from the body and sprinkled on the altar. In chapter 17, verses 10–11, it says,

> "And every man of the house of Israel and of the sojourner who sojourns in their midst who consumes any blood, I shall set My face against the living person who consumes blood and cut him off from the midst of his people. For the life of the flesh is in the blood. And as for Me, I have given it to you on the altar to ransom your lives, for it is the blood that ransoms in exchange for life. Therefore have I said to the Israelites; no living person among you shall consume blood, nor shall the sojourner who sojourns in your midst consume blood."

Even if you are out hunting and kill some animal, you are to drain out the blood and cover it with dust. This order not to eat or drink blood is repeated in various forms several times in Leviticus, in addition to references in Genesis and Exodus.

It was a big deal. Blood was to be drained off, maybe used as part of the sacrificial ritual, but never eaten or drunk. Sacrificial altars seemed to have had a special groove to drain the blood away. Part of having an animal meet the kosher rules is that the blood is drained as completely as possible. Not eating or drinking blood was a big deal in Jewish law, right up there with not murdering people.

Yet here we have Jesus telling his disciples to drink his blood, even if it was really wine. And there's no record of anybody saying, "Uh, Jesus, uh, you know, that's not really kosher." Drinking blood was so out of bounds to a Jew that you have to wonder what was really going on. Did this really happen? Did these men, most of whom probably considered themselves good Jews through the rest of their lives, just say, "Well, it's really just wine, so it's not like we're really breaking the law of God. We're only spiritually or symbolically breaking the most basic dietary law, so God won't really turn against us"? Something is going on here that is a mystery of the first order.

Why would Jesus institute a rite that seems to transgress a fundamental tenet of Judaism? Was he that desperate to come up with a symbol saying he was the source of life? And why did everybody seem to just go along, including Paul, the Pharisee of the Pharisees? What is the power, the meaning, of this ritual that violates the basic law of God? Jesus telling his disciples to drink his blood, even if only symbolically, goes against everything ingrained into these men and seems to break away from the very basis of Judaism, yet nobody in the early church seems to object, even when it caused outsiders to accuse them of cannibalism. How is this possible?

I guess you are all sitting here expecting me to answer those questions. But I told you at the beginning it was a mystery, and so it remains.

Amen.

Sermon Seven

God

I would like to propose a new definition for God. I would like us to at least consider the idea that God is that which creates. To put it another way, whatever it is that creates, that is God, no matter what that turns out to be. Now, I know we usually think of God as "the Creator," but we tend to think of that as a characteristic of God, like being powerful or eternal. We say, "God cares," "God controls," "God creates." I want to flip that and see what happens if we say that being God is a characteristic of whatever it is that creates.

Now, those of us who grew up in a monotheistic religion may have a little trouble thinking about anything that doesn't create being a god, but that was actually one of Paul's knocks against the Greek and Roman gods; they were not the creators of the world. Paul's argument was that people should know who the real God is because they saw the power of God in his creation every day. These other gods—Zeus and Jupiter and the others—couldn't be real gods because they did not create the world, and the god of the Jews was the creator.

For example, the Greek creation story was that originally everything was a nothingness called Chaos. Somehow Gaia, the earth, emerged, along with some other divine beings such as Eros (Love), the Abyss called Tartarus, and Erebus (Darkness). Even without a male around, Gaia somehow gives birth to the sky, called Uranus, who then fertilizes Gaia. Gaia then gives birth to twelve Titans, including a schemer called Cronus.

Cronus arranges to have his father, Uranus, castrated, and despite being the youngest Titan, Cronus takes over as king of the Titans. He marries his sister Rhea and has a bunch of children, but he's afraid one of his children will do to him what he did to his father, so as soon as they are born, he eats them. Rhea gets a little tired of this after a while and tricks Cronus by wrapping a stone in a baby blanket and passing the rock off as the baby, so Cronus swallows the stone, blanket and all.

This baby god who survived is named Zeus, and when he grows up, he slips Cronus a drug that makes him vomit, and all the other baby gods Cronus ate come back up, along with the stone. Cronus and the Titans go to war with Zeus and his brothers and sisters, Zeus and his team win, Cronus and the other Titans are tossed into the Abyss as a prison, and Zeus takes over as king of the Gods.

The point of this gruesome, and very simplified, little story, as far as we are concerned, is that the gods the Greeks were worshipping when Paul was wandering around—Zeus, Hera, Athena, etc.—were not even first-generation gods; they were third and fourth generation descendants of the original creators. The Romans worshipped basically these same gods under different names.

This idea that the gods currently in charge of the world were not the ones who made it was actually not uncommon. The Egyptians had several versions of a creation story, but, basically, there was a lifeless water of chaos called Nu; a mound emerged from the water, then the sun, Ra or Atum, rose from the mound. After that, the story sort of depends on where in Egypt you live, but one version is that Atum masturbates to produce Shu and Tefnut (Air and Space), who mate to produce Geb and Nut (Earth and Sky), who have the children who get most of the attention in the temples—Osiris, Isis, Set, and Nephthys.

The Indo-Europeans seemed to have a slightly different idea of creation since Indo-European cultures as widely separated as the Norse and the Hindus have the idea not that god created, but that the body of a god—Ymir for the Norse and Brahman for the Hindu—was dismembered into pieces to create the world, the other gods, animals, and human beings. Now, where that original god who got all chopped up came from isn't exactly clear. The *Rig Veda* puts it this way, talking about Brahman:

> Who really knows, and who can swear,
> How creation came, when or where!
> Even gods came after creation's day,
> Who really knows, who can truly say
> When and how did creation start?
> Did He do it? Or did He not?
> Only He, up there, knows, maybe;
> Or perhaps, not even He.
> — *Rig Veda* 10:129:1–7

So, this idea Paul was pushing of a Creator God who was still running the show, an idea that grew out of the theology of the Hebrews over the years, was actually different from what was going around in other cultures of the time.

Now, if you read the Old Testament really carefully, you see that this idea of there only being one God, who was the creator and still in charge, was not totally there from the beginning, even for the Hebrews. Even in the Ten Commandments, when it orders, "You shall have no other gods before me," it seems to be admitting there are other gods. Psalm 82 talks about God meeting with a council of the gods. Even one of the words for God, "Elohim," is actually plural in ancient Hebrew, though it's used with both plural and singular verbs in the Old Testament, just to make things more confusing. Genesis talks about the "sons of gods" in Genesis 6:2. Elohim is actually probably somehow related to the Canaanite language, probably derived from another name for god, "El," who was the creator god and main God of the Canaanite Pantheon of gods.

The differences between the Canaanites and the Hebrews were somewhere between slim and nonexistent way, way back, which is why they were such bitter enemies later on as the Hebrews in the highlands gradually became more attracted to this idea of a single, all-powerful, creator god while the Canaanites down on the plain stuck with their multiple gods like El, Baal, Asherah, and Moloch, who make multiple appearances in the Bible as the gods the Hebrews were always going back to.

But anyway, this idea of one god who was creator and everything else, and all the other gods nothing but fictions come up with to explain the forces of nature and life, was not a common idea back then but something that grew slowly over time in one little group in the highlands between the Mediterranean and the Dead Seas. But it eventually took over so much once Christianity became the dominant religion that those of us today who have trouble thinking of God as anything other than "Creator" are going to have to stretch a bit to think of it as the other way around—as whatever creates being God.

But we have to stop here and take a step back and admit that we are making a huge assumption. We are assuming that there was a creation. We're so used to things like the Genesis story and the Big Bang that the idea that the universe could just be, instead of becoming, might seem a little strange. But we talk about God "just being," without beginning or end, eternal in both directions. I'm not sure there's any logical reason other things couldn't "just be" as well. Certainly, the Bible talks about Jesus being there at the beginning, and maybe before, though this Trinity idea makes all that a little confusing, and there are certainly references to things like Wisdom, called Sophia, and the angels being around. If God could just be, maybe other things could just be too.

As for the Big Bang, that seems pretty obvious now, but people forget that back in the 1900s there was a long argument about the Big Bang versus what was called a "steady-state universe," a universe that didn't begin, it just was, is, and will be. The evidence slowly accumulated that supported the Big Bang, so the steady-state universe was swept into the dustbin of scientific history, but then the question became what happens in the future.

Some people thought there would be a "Big Crunch" at the other end of the line, with the universe compressing into a singularity like it was at the start of the Big Bang. And then maybe it would just recycle and start all over. Right now, the math is more in favor of a "Big Freeze," where the universe keeps expanding until everything gets so far apart that no new stars get created, the existing stars burn out, even the black holes eventually evaporate when they run out of stars to absorb, and the universe becomes nothing but frozen space full of nothing, shooting off away from all other spaces full of nothing to the point they don't even affect each other anymore. Now, that's so far down the road that none of us can even conceive of the timescale, not to mention need to worry about it, but it's an interesting philosophical exercise to ask, *What is the purpose of creating a universe that is going to end up cold, empty, and dead?*

But back to creation. Where did the Big Bang come from anyway? One of the hardest things to understand about the Big

Bang is that that question makes no sense. Time, like space, is part of the universe. I know we usually think of the Big Bang as this tiny dot sitting in empty space that suddenly explodes, but that's wrong. Before the Big Bang, there was no space for a dot to sit in. Space, dimension, up, down, height, depth, width, all were created in the Big Bang. To ask how wide the singularity of the Big Bang was is not just an unanswerable question, it is an illogical question because width did not exist. In just the same way, time did not exist. There was no "before" before. The idea of before the Big Bang, or where did the Big Bang come from, is meaningless. Creation not only started the clock, it started what clocks measure.

Speaking of clocks, and getting back to ideas that don't totally blow our minds, I want to make it clear that what I am proposing is not quite the old "Clockmaker" or "Watchmaker" view of creation and the universe. Back when Newtonian mechanics was state-of-the-art physics, the idea was popular that the universe was like a complex but very accurate clock or watch, all the pieces moving precisely—which, of course, meant if you have a great clock, you have to have a great clockmaker; that precise clocks don't just happen by chance, you have to have somebody putting all these complex pieces together. The universe had to be made by an extremely skilled creator who understood exactly how everything worked together and put it together piece by piece.

By extension, we could look at the universe and see the mind of God, how ordered and exactly everything fitted together, reflecting the structure of how God thought. There was even the belief that if you could ever know the exact position and velocity of every particle in the universe, and had one heck of a computer, you could calculate exactly where every one of those particles had been in the past and would be in the future. That was not practical, of course, but it shows how people used to think of the universe—as a very precise instrument with a fixed past and future.

Now, what I'm saying is that the logic here is not totally invalid. The universe, the Creation, should be able to tell us something about that which creates. But we can't assume God. We have to get the order right. Creation tells us about "that which creates," and we have to accept whatever *that* turns out to be as God, not the other way around.

Of course, one problem is that we have eventually figured out that the universe is not very much like a clock. Or if it is, it's a pretty lousy clock. It's messy, uncertain, not something that you necessarily want to bet the farm on. Einstein famously said that God does not play dice with the universe, but it turns out that was one of the few things he was wrong about. The universe is very much like a game of craps, a roll of the dice, a game of chance. In the first place, this idea that you could know the exact position and speed and direction of even one particle has been shot out of the water. If you know where something is, you don't know exactly how fast it's going or in what direction. If you do measure exactly how fast and where a particle is going, you can't know exactly where it is to start with. There is always an element of uncertainty.

And when two particles interact, it gets even more complicated. What comes out of all this is a crapshoot. Like rolling dice, I can tell you exactly the odds, the probability, of getting a certain number—a six or a seven, say, on any given roll. And if you roll the dice a trillion times, I can tell you almost exactly how many of those rolls will be a seven. But if you want to know if this particular roll will be a seven, I have no idea. All I can do is give you the odds. What is actually going to happen is unknowable until it actually happens and you look to see which number came up.

It turns out the universe pretty much works that way. For any little event, like two atoms colliding, there are certain probabilities of what might happen, but no certainty. For lots of big things, involving lots of events, the odds build up and get pretty close to certainty, but there is always at least one wild chance that something else will happen. And if you roll the dice enough, over and over, trillions of times for years on end, sooner or later the dice will end up propped against each other, balanced on their corners. Given time, even the most unlikely sequence of events will occur, and sometimes this sets off other chains of events that move up the scale, and new patterns emerge, new relationships, so that chance could create this crazy little jury-rigged universe.

So the universe is like that—you can calculate the odds and bet on the near certainties, but sooner or later, something really weird will pop up. There is even a theory that every time the universe has one of these little events, every time it rolls the dice, reality splits to cover all the possible outcomes, no matter how unlikely, resulting in an almost infinite number of "many worlds." We just happen to live in the universe that led to us, with millions more universes being created every instant. How you would ever be able to tell if this theory is true and what difference it would make if you could isn't clear, but it's just another example of creation being possibly much different from what we thought it was.

So, what can we say about creation? Well, if the Big Freeze is where we're headed, it all seems sort of pointless. After all, what good does it do to create a universe if all you're going to get in the end is endless empty frozen space? Maybe it is the trip and not the destination, but it still seems like a strange destination. Even if it turns out to be a Big Crunch, still, what's the point?

Singularity to singularity, from nothing to nothing. Either way, I guess we can forget about any monuments to mankind at the end of the universe. We won't be around either way, but it still makes you wonder.

Another thing about creation is that nothing is certain. It's all playing the odds. Chance rules the universe. Some outcomes are more probable than others, sometimes a lot more probable, but there is always a joker in the deck, to change gambling metaphors. We need to adjust ourselves to the idea that cause and effect is not necessarily a one-to-one relationship—that a single cause probably will have a specific effect—but it just might cause something else, that much-less-likely effect.

Third, creation encompasses much more than we usually think. We think about creation as humans and animals, earth and sky, planets and stars. But it also includes space and time, energy and matter. Like the people of the past who had to adjust their thinking from the earth being the center of the universe to being a planet going around the sun, to the stars being other suns, to all these suns going around the center of a galaxy, to the earth being a little planet going around an average sun out in the backwoods of a spiral arm of a galaxy that is just one of trillions of galaxies full of gazillions of stars with bazillions of planets, we are going to have to adjust our thinking to include space and time as part of creation, not eternals. Perhaps creation itself is not eternal. Or more precisely, perhaps eternity is not a concept we can apply to creation, eternity being too limited an idea to use to describe that which creates.

And if that which creates is God, what can we say about God? We can say that if God has a plan for the universe, we don't see it. And if that which creates is God, God is a major league gambler, constantly playing the odds, and we're not real sure we can tell when God wins and when God loses. And if that which creates is God, we have a far too small and limited idea of God.

Whatever it is that creates, creates much more than we have even dreamed. If we human beings are the reason for the existence of the universe, there is a whole heck of a lot of universe out there that we will never be a part of. Space and time, not just the universe, are part of creation; is that all for us? And is there really only just one universe? Our idea of God is far too small, far too limited.

We understand neither the purpose nor the point of creation. Creation is full of uncertainty and chance. And creation is far, far more than our wildest thoughts. And I think it's time we stop claiming we know what God wants, or what God can and cannot do, and start listening to the universe and its echoes of creation.

Amen.

Acknowledgments

I wish to thank Rev. Dr. G. Oliver Wagner and especially Rev. Caitlin Phillips for their thoughtful comments and suggestions.

As usual, I thank my wife, Kathy, and my daughter, Elizabeth, for their support.

About the Author

David Davis has had one book published—a science fiction novel entitled *The Mistakes*, published by Kohler Books in 2020. In addition, he has had seventeen plays produced, including productions in New York and Hollywood. His script, *Night of the Hawk*, was produced off-off Broadway in 2003. He has also had several poems, magazine features, and scholarly articles published. He earned a PhD in theater and is a member of the Dramatists Guild and Working Title Playwrights. He has worked as a physics and math teacher, actor, head of three college theater programs, technical writer, editor, and health communications specialist. He currently lives in Atlanta, Georgia, with his wife, Kathy, and has one daughter, Elizabeth.